"*Be Killing Sin* is a heart-penetrating read and profitable for both new and seasoned believers who sincerely desire to be exhorted regarding the danger of personal sin and educated in the biblical means of defeating sin in their lives. I highly recommend Dr. Steele's uncompromising and practical book on this much-needed topic."

STEVE BALVANZ, Senior Pastor, Spring Creek Bible Church, Bellingham, WA

"Dr. David Steele's book, *Be Killing Sin*, is an excellent reminder of how every believer ought to live the Christian life on a daily basis. Pastor David provides a strategic blueprint for 'fighting the good fight of faith,' while standing against the world, the flesh, and the devil with God's armor in place. In addition to the clear biblical teaching that permeates this book, David also provides a treasure-chest of valuable quotes, references, and biblical truths that you will want to access time and again. I highly recommend that you add this book to your library and read it repeatedly to fortify your soul against the temptations and struggles we all have with sin."

BRUCE PARKER, Pastor Emeritus, Faith Bible Church, Hood River, OR

"I was discipled as a young Christian under the ministry of David Steele. For years, I witnessed his life and sat under his faithful preaching and teaching. I know no man who is more well-read, self-disciplined, or biblically and theologically astute. For decades, one of Pastor Dave's specialties has been apologetics and engagement with cultural issues, teaching followers of Jesus to be discerning, "thinking Christianly," and living for the glory of God in all that they do. So, what you'll receive in *Be Killing Sin* is guidance that is as biblically grounded as it gets, and which speaks practically to the issues of sin in our culture and in our hearts. If you need help in the fight against sin (and we all do), 'take up and read!'"

BROCK EWING, Senior Pastor, Homestead Country Gathering, La Grande, OR

"With the skill of a surgeon, from the hand of a seasoned pastor-teacher of God's Word, and the mind of a scholar, David Steele has gifted the Church with a magnificent and needed book in *Be Killing Sin: The Art of War on the Battlefield of Faith*. Whether you think sin is a "little matter" or a grave matter, this book is needed in a day that devalues sin and focuses on psychological aspects of our humanity, which causes us to look first to ourselves, or worse, to find a cure that isn't possible outside of Christ. Wherever you are at on that spectrum, I encourage you to read this book, to be taught from Scripture about sin, the glory of Christ, and how putting on Christ in all of life is not some part of the Christian life; it is the whole of the Christian life because of our union with Christ."

DAVE JENKINS, Executive Director, Servants of Grace Ministries, Executive Director, Theology for Life Magazine, Host, Equipping You in Grace, Author, The Word Explored and the Word Matters.

"Dr. Steele's book, *Be Killing Sin* is a book that I hope will not fall on deaf ears. It has arrived at a strategic time as the contemporary church tends to minimize the subject of sin or avoid it entirely. I recommend everyone to read this book, especially church leaders."

KEN CHIN, Talis Biomedical, Milpitas, CA

"I have great hope that *Be Killing Sin* will be a blessing to the church. I love David's obvious zeal for the Lord and his infectious desire to see individual Christians as well as the church as a whole walk faithfully before the Lord and serve as lights to the world."

PETE WILLIAMSON, Great Commandments Ministry, Yakima, WA

Be Killing Sin

David S. Steele

ISBN: 9798841405030

To my children,

Abigail Noël and Nathan David

May you always hate sin and pursue God with unrelenting passion and zeal. May your deep love of God and the gospel of his Son fuel every decision and embolden every action. And may you walk by the power of the Holy Spirit, giving glory to God in all things.

But the steadfast love of the LORD is from everlasting to everlasting on those who fear him, and his righteousness to children's children, to those who keep his covenant and remember to do his commandments. (Psalm 103:17–18)

Contents

Introduction

Desmond T. Doss was the unassuming hero of the motion picture, *Hacksaw Ridge*. The movie tells the true tale of a man who willingly wore the uniform and served his nation after the Japanese invasion of Pearl Harbor. Driven by a love for God and country, Doss enlisted in the United States military to help defend the cause of freedom. Yet, he was motivated by an unconventional core conviction. This conviction ran against the prevailing military wisdom, as he refused to accept a weapon.

Doss was not blinded by the lure of military fame. Nor was he playing some kind of game for publicity. On the contrary, he had every intention of helping his fellow soldiers by administering medical care on the battlefield. "He had come into the Army willingly," writes Booton Herndon, "but as a conscientious objector, a non-combatant. Though eager to serve his country, he had the written assurance of the President of the United States Franklin D. Roosevelt through Executive Order Number 8606 and the Chief of Staff of the Army that he would not have to bear arms."[1] But sometimes Executive Orders are not carried out in a way that is in sync with our desires. Such was the case with Desmond T. Doss.

Doss was placed in the 77th Infantry Division, the last place a conscientious objector wishes to serve. So, this soldier faced a serious dilemma in his refusal to accept a weapon, in keeping with his convictions. His superiors demanded that he take hold of a firearm. But Doss was no wavering warrior. There would be no fighting for this unorthodox military man. There would be no shooting. There would certainly be no killing on the battlefield. This young soldier stood his ground and refused to lay his hands on a weapon.

Providentially, Doss was moved to a medical battalion where he could tend to the physical needs of his brothers in the combat zone. First Lieutenant Onless C. Brister speaks in glowing terms about this non-conformist soldier: "Private Doss was at all times up with the front lines to care for injured men. In several instances, he braved intense enemy small arms and mortar fire to give aid and to move men who were wounded."[2] This soldier, who refused to fight, served his country with honor and distinction. And he saved seventy-five lives without ever carrying a gun.

We oftentimes hear that President Reagan won the Cold War without a shot being fired. Doss could certainly sympathize with this steely heroism. On October 12, 1945, President Harry Truman awarded Desmond T. Doss with the Medal of Honor, the first conscientious objector to receive such a distinction.

Battling Spiritual Pacifism

While we rightly applaud Doss for standing firm and living according to his convictions, we must confess that some of us as Christians adopt a similar strategy in our "fight" against sin. Like Doss, many of us refuse to take up arms and fight with faithful resolve. We turn away from the weapons at our disposal, namely, prayer and the Word of God. And we are ignorant of the biblical command to wage holy warfare against sin. The result is a life filled with guilt, regret, and spiritual defeat.

But spiritual pacifism is never an option for a follower of Jesus Christ. In his masterful work, *The Christian Warrior: Wrestling with Sin, Satan, the World and the Flesh*, Isaac Ambrose (1604-1664) challenges Christian warriors:

> Soldiers of Christ, be aware that you are highly advanced in God's creation, that you occupy an important station, that you have an arduous work allotted to you, and that you have neither time nor talent to throw away. For you are enlisted under the banner of Christ, you have entered the armies of the Most High, and have taken the oath of allegiance to the King of Zion, and bound yourselves by an oath, to fight the good fight of faith, against sin, Satan, the world and the flesh.[3]

Like a soldier in the United States military who takes an oath to "support and defend the Constitution of the United States against all enemies, foreign and domestic," so too does the follower of Christ swear his or her allegiance to fighting the good fight to the glory of God. This fight entails a lifelong battle with sin that doesn't end until we reach the shores of the Celestial City.

Tragically, however, this is not often the case. Let's face it, many of us are spiritual pacifists. We are spiritual cowards. We resist the fight against sin and show ourselves to be spiritual weaklings. And when we refuse to don the spiritual armor and fight the fight of faith, our passivity bears withered fruit that fails to honor God. Spiritual pacifism is a losing battle that is inconsistent with our high calling in Jesus Christ.

Battling the Reality of Sin

Some professing Christians have moved beyond spiritual pacifism and have become experts at ignoring sin altogether. The late Robert Schuller is a classic example. His view of sin was essentially a "lack of self-esteem." Schuller argues, "Sin is psychological self-abuse ... the most serious sin is one that causes me to say, 'I am unworthy. I may have no claim to divine sonship if you examine me at my worst.' Once a person believes he is an 'unworthy sinner,' it is doubtful if he can really honestly accept the saving grace God offers in Jesus Christ."[4] Schuller's view of sin may initially appear to boost the ego, but it fails, in the final analysis, to adequately explain the human condition and leaves sinners in a spiritual wasteland where hope is nowhere to be found.

In Paul Young's recent book, *Lies We Believe About God*, he does not ignore sin but redefines it: "Blind, not depraved, is our condition," writes Young.[5] He continues, "Sin, then, is anything that negates or diminishes or misrepresents the truth of who you are, no matter how pretty or ugly that is."[6] Such a view finds no biblical support and is a foreign concept in Christian theology.

Young acknowledges that sin involves "missing the mark." But he adds, "The mark is not perfect moral behavior. The 'mark' is the Truth of your being."[7] But Young goes one step further in his redefinition of sin: "And what does the truth of your being look like? God. You are made in the image of God, and the truth of your being looks like God."[8]

Discerning readers will note that while Young nibbles around the edges of orthodoxy by paying lip service to biblical terminology, his articulation of Christian theology, in the end, falls dreadfully short and fails to honor Scripture. It turns out that Young actually misrepresents sin and like Schuller, leaves the sinner languishing in the same spiritual wasteland. Instead of helping people move forward with God-centered resolve in the Christian life, Young's view hinders them by failing to tell the truth about their true condition.

John MacArthur observes that people have difficulty coming to grips with their sinful condition: "They don't want to face it. They try to eliminate that sense of guilt by adopting a more convenient kind of morality, or by silencing their crying consc ience."[9] That's exactly what we've seen in the examples above.

Sweeping sin under the rug or minimizing its tragic influence in our lives is not only wrong-headed, it's just plain foolish. Cornelius Plantinga Jr. reminds us that, "self-deception about our sin is a narcotic, a tranquilizing and disorienting suppression of our spiritual central nervous system."[10] We've learned that it is safer to keep our heads in the sand; that playing the role of an ostrich is easier and more convenient than exercising vigilance and biblical discernment. And when we fail to face up to our sin, we are simply unable to hear the claims of the gospel or fight sin with biblical faithfulness.

Belittling the Seriousness of Sin

Dr. Karl Menninger is perplexed that the notion of sin has slowly vanished:

> In all the laments and reproaches made by our seers and prophets, one misses any mention of 'sin,' a word which used to be a veritable watchword of prophets. It was a word once in everyone's mind, but now rarely if ever heard. Does that mean that no sin is involved in all our troubles - sin with an 'I' in the middle? Is no one any longer guilty of anything? Guilty perhaps of a sin that could be repented and repaired or atoned for? Is it only that someone may be stupid or sick or criminal - or asleep? Wrong things are being done, we know; tares are being sown in the wheat field at night. But is no one responsible, no one answerable for these acts? Anxiety and depression we all acknowledge, and even vague guilt feelings; but has no one committed any sins? Where, indeed, did sin go? What became of it? [11]

All this is to say that it appears we are no longer taking sin seriously. We have lost our moral compass, which is to suggest that we have wandered off the path; we have lost our way. "True north" has transformed into whatever our desires dictate. The unchanging truth of God's Word no longer grips our hearts and informs our minds. And the "boa constrictor" of moral relativism has us by the throat. Israel reached this low point and the tragic consequences are written for all to see:

> Woe to those who draw iniquity with cords of falsehood, who draw sin as with cart ropes, who say: 'Let him be quick, let him speed his work that we may see it; let the counsel of the Holy One of Israel draw near, and let it come, that we may know it!' Woe to those who call evil good and good evil, who put darkness for light and light for darkness, who put bitter for sweet and sweet for bitter! Woe to those who are wise in their own eyes, and shrewd in their own sight! Woe to those who are heroes at drinking wine, and valiant men in mixing strong drink, who acquit the guilty for a bribe, and deprive the innocent of his right! Therefore, as the tongue of fire devours the stubble, and as dry grass sinks down in the flame, so their root will be as rottenness, and their blossom go up like dust; for they have rejected the law of the Lord of hosts, and have despised the word of the Holy One of Israel. Therefore the anger of the Lord was kindled against his people, and he stretched out his hand against them and struck them, and the mountains quaked; and their corpses were as refuse in the midst of the streets. For all this his anger has not turned away, and his hand is stretched out still. (Isa. 5:18–25)

Like Israel, we have reached the point of critical mass in the contemporary church as we fail to take sin seriously. The consequences are sobering, and the fallout is far from over. At one level, it is rather easy to see the signs of a church that refuses to take sin seriously. For example, there was a day when the church confronted the sin of divorce; now many churches condone it. There was a day when the church admonished the sin of gluttony; now many churches gloss over it. There was a day when the sin of homosexuality was addressed with direct and compassionate biblical counseling; now many churches either minimize it or allow it. Some churches even celebrate this grievous sin. And the sin of pornography is given "a pass" while men of all ages sink deeper and deeper into unbridled defeat and depravity. Surely, the next generation will pay a heavy price as the contemporary church allows sin to penetrate her walls and pulverize the people of God.

These are troubling developments, but they should not surprise us. God's Word calls our attention to this kind of gross immorality and godlessness, which will dominate the last days:

> For people will be lovers of self, lovers of money, proud, arrogant, abusive, disobedient to their parents, ungrateful, unholy, heartless, unappeasable, slanderous, without self-control, brutal, not loving good, treacherous, reckless, swollen with conceit, lovers of pleasure rather than lovers of God, having the appearance of godliness, but denying its power. Avoid such people. (2 Tim. 3:2–5)

This refusal to take sin seriously may be easy enough to diagnose but the blatant disregard for holiness, in the end, shakes us to the core. This casual attitude toward sin may cause faithful followers of Christ to be discouraged and suffer loss along the way.

However, at another level, the repudiation of the doctrine of sin is far more subtle. For instance, as I gaze upon thousands of books in my study, I see whole sections devoted to different theological categories. I see a section on the Trinity, Christology (the doctrine of Christ), Pneumatology (the doctrine of the Holy Spirit), Soteriology (the doctrine of salvation), Ecclesiology (the doctrine of the church), Eschatology (the doctrine of last things), and many others. Yet, there is a distinct lack of books on Hamartiology (the doctrine of sin).

The devil is perfectly happy to see the doctrine of sin slide into the sea of forgetfulness. He is delighted when professing Christians minimize sin or redefine it. Uncle Screwtape, C.S. Lewis's senior demon in *The Screwtape Letters* observed that the journey to hell is found in mere passivity: "Indeed the safest road to Hell is the gradual one - the gentle slope, soft underfoot, without sudden turnings, without milestones, without sign-posts."[12] When we belittle the seriousness of sin, we become easy prey for the enemy of our souls.

Be Killing Sin

Sinclair Ferguson tells a touching tale about a pastor who greeted him at the end of a church conference. He asked, "Just before I let you go tonight, will you do one last thing? Will you take me through the steps that are involved so that we learn to mortify sin?"[13] This powerful question deserves a serious answer that finds its origin in Scripture.

My goal in this book is to guide you on a journey that *exposes* the vicious monster of sin, *explains* the posture in our battle with sin, and *expounds* on a plan to defeat it. We will not rest until we learn how to deal with sin decisively and biblically.

Part one will expose *the pathology of sin*. Our task will be to unveil and lay sin bare. In doing so, we will trace the many ways that sin wreaks havoc in our lives. Here, we will explore the origin of sin, the nature of sin, and see how some are repudiating the biblical definition of sin.

Part two explains *the powerful safeguard in our fight against sin*. It will provide a helpful summary of the never-ending battle we face in the Christian life. We will turn to the apostle Paul, who will outfit us with the necessary armor for the ensuing war.

Part three will expound on *a plan for defeating sin* with the help of the Puritans. One noted Puritan theologian, John Owen said, "Be killing sin, or sin will be killing you." His wisdom along with other Puritan divines served believers in the 17th century and continue to provide believers with the necessary fuel for battling sin in our generation.

Be Killing Sin is written with the new believer in mind but will encourage seasoned believers as well. "The uniqueness and the glory of the New Testament path of sanctification, and the power to kill sin (Rom. 8:13), is that this path is walked, and this warfare is fought, by those who have been once for all justified by faith alone."[14] As we move forward, may we follow in the sin-slaying path that John Owen made so clear and practical. May we heed the words of the apostle Peter:

> Therefore, preparing your minds for action, and being sober-minded, set your hope fully on the grace that will be brought to you at the revelation of Jesus Christ. As obedient children, do not be conformed to the passions of your former ignorance, but as he who called you is holy, you also be holy in all your conduct, since it is written, 'You shall be holy, for I am holy.' (1 Pet. 1:13–16)

And may we be encouraged by the godly foot soldiers whose shoulders we stand on, men who have helped pave the way and encourage us to fight the good fight:

> While in the heat of the battle, be filled with the hope of victory, and feel assured, that you shall finally obtain a complete and glorious conquest over all that come against you; for hath not the Captain of your salvation engaged to subdue Satan and all his armies, shortly under your feet? Trust him, and take courage, then, you cannot meet with disappointment, 'for faithful is he that promised, who also will do it.'[15]

---

1. Booton Herndon, Hero of Hacksaw Ridge (Goldwater: Remnant Publications, Inc., 2016), 7.
2. Cited in Ibid., 91.
3. Isaac Ambrose, The Christian Warrior: Wrestling with Sin, Satan, the World and the Flesh (Digital Puritan Press, 2012), Kindle edition, Loc. 34.
4. Robert Schuller, Self-Esteem: The New Reformation (Waco: Word Books, 1982), 98.
5. WM. Paul Young, Lies We Believe About God (New York: Atria Books, 2017), Kindle edition, Loc. 296.
6. Ibid., Loc. 1645.
7. Ibid., Loc. 1643.
8. Ibid., Loc. 1645.
9. John MacArthur, The Gospel According to Paul: Embracing the Good News at the Heart of Paul's Teachings (Nashville: Thomas Nelson, 2017), 27.
10. Cornelius Plantinga Jr., Not the Way It's Supposed to Be: A Breviary of Sin (Grand Rapids: Eerdmans Publishing Company, 1995), xiii.
11. Karl Menninger, Whatever Became of Sin? (New York: Hawthorn, 1973), 13. Cited in John MacArthur, The Vanishing Conscience (Dallas: Word Publishing, 1994), 17.

12. C.S. Lewis, The Screwtape Letters (New York: Macmillan Publishing Company, 1982), 56.
13. Sinclair Ferguson, Some Pastors and Teachers (Edinburgh: Banner of Truth, 2017), 763.
14. John Piper, What is Saving Faith? (Wheaton: Crossway Books, 2022), 84.
15. Isaac Ambrose, The Christian Warrior: Wrestling with Sin, Satan, the World and the Flesh, Kindle edition, Loc. 44.

PART I: THE PATHOLOGY OF SIN

"PATHOLOGY" DESCRIBES THE CAUSES and effects of a particular disease. For example, it is generally accepted that smoking cigarettes may very well lead to lung cancer. According to the *American Cancer Society*, tobacco use is the leading preventable cause of death in the US, accounting for about 1 in 5 deaths each year.[1] Research suggests:

- Smoking causes about 20% of all cancers and about 30% of all cancer deaths in the United States.
- About 80% of lung cancers, as well as about 80% of all lung cancer deaths, are due to smoking.
- Lung cancer is the leading cause of cancer death in both men and women.

With those odds, it is a great mystery why anyone would willingly place a cigarette between their lips! The sobering prospects of smoking should motivate even the most ardent proponent of tobacco to think twice before inhaling.

In the early stages, cigarette smoke begins to slowly wreak havoc on the human body. At first, the physical effects are minimal, but a slow erosion is taking place to the unsuspecting smoker. The *American Cancer Society* reports, "Smoking damages the airways and small air sacs" in the lungs.[2] While it may take time, in some cases many years, the effects take a horrible toll on the lungs, and disease is often the result. The effects of a disease like cancer are tragic indeed, as patients battle intense pain and struggle to breathe.

But the risk of contracting cancer is only the tip of the iceberg for smokers. A host of other physical problems await those who choose to inhale, including chronic obstructive pulmonary disease (COPD) and emphysema, to name a few.

Knowing both the causes and effects of a given disease will help us understand what we're up against and the great lengths we need to go to in fighting the disease.

The pathology of the "sin disease" is our focus in part one. Here, we will witness the genesis of sin and the devastating effects it has on human beings. In the classic film, *The Wizard of Oz*, Dorothy and her friends were urged to "follow the yellow brick road." What they discovered at the end of the road was a harmless wizard. What we discover in part one will be anything but harmless.

Our task in part one is to unveil sin and expose this vicious monster. As we expose the pathology of sin, we will see:

- The origin of sin
- The nature and extent of sin
- The repudiation of sin

Brace yourself as we move forward into enemy territory. Our journey will be devastating, but a necessary pursuit in order to make progress in our fight against sin.

---

1. www.cancer.org.
2. Ibid.

1

The Origin of Sin

For when we realize that Satan is busy and at his tricks, then we are on our guard; then we seek refuge in Him who has crushed Satan's head; then we close our hearts to the stealthy, murderous enemy.

ABRAHAM KUYPER

God created the universe in six days. Scripture repeatedly affirms the "goodness" of creation (Gen. 1:10, 12, 21, 25). On the sixth day, God made man: "So God created man in his own image, in the image of God he created him; male and female he created them" (Gen. 1:27). Once again, the goodness of creation is affirmed: "And God saw everything that he had made, and behold, it was very good ..." (Gen. 1:31).

Genesis 2:4 reaffirms the creative work of God: "These are the generations of the heavens and the earth when they were created, in the day that the LORD God made the earth and the heavens." God charges Adam with stewarding his good creation: "The LORD God took the man and put him in the garden of Eden to work it and keep it" (Gen. 2:15). Additionally, God utters a critical command that Adam is duty-bound to obey: "And the LORD God commanded the man, saying, 'You may surely eat of every tree of the garden, but of the tree of the knowledge of good and evil you shall not eat, for in the day that you eat of it you shall surely die'" (Gen. 2:16-17).

Eve is fashioned out of one of Adam's ribs by the creative hand of God and the covenant of marriage is established in clear and unmistakable terms: "Therefore a man shall leave his father and his mother and hold fast to his wife, and they shall become one flesh. And the man and his wife were both naked and were not ashamed" (Gen. 2:24-25).

A perfect God creates a perfect world, whose aim is to glorify the greatness of his worth. "Everyone who is called by my name, whom I created for my glory" (Isa. 43:7). The creatures that God fashioned enjoyed fellowship with each other, and they enjoyed unhindered worship of God. Everything was perfect until the serpent slithered into the garden and questioned the wisdom of the Creator: "Did God actually say, 'You shall not eat of any tree in the garden?'" (Gen. 3:1b). The woman listened to his God-dishonoring question and responded to his asinine assertion: "You will not surely die. For God knows that when you eat of it your eyes will be opened, and you will be like God, knowing good and evil (Gen. 3:4-5). Scripture says that she was deceived by the devil's cunning (2 Cor. 11:3). *Cunning* (*panourgia*) is best translated as "duplicity," "craftiness," "trickery," or "villainy." The serpent used his evil devices to deceive the woman.

The Westminster Confession of Faith captures the seductive nature of the original sin: "Our first parents being seduced by the subtlety and temptation of Satan, sinned in eating the forbidden fruit. This their sin God was pleased, according to his wise and holy counsel, to permit having purposed to order it to his own glory."[1] Eve believed his pernicious lie: "So when the woman saw that the tree was good for food, and that it was a delight to the eyes, and that the tree was to be desired to make one wise, she took of its fruit and ate, and she also gave some to her husband who was with her, and he ate" (Gen. 3:6).

The sin of our first parents sent humanity on a downward spiral that resulted in a curse that directly affected the serpent and all of humanity. God said to the serpent:

> Because you have done this, cursed are you above all livestock and above all beasts of the field; on your belly you shall go, and dust you shall eat all the days of your life. I will put enmity between you and the woman and between your offspring and her offspring; he shall bruise your head and you shall bruise his heel. (Gen. 3:14-15)

God said to the woman:

> I will surely multiply your pain in childbearing; in pain you shall bring forth children. Your desire shall be for your husband, and he shall rule over you. (Gen. 3:16)

To Adam, God said:

> Because you have listened to the voice of your wife and have eaten of the tree of which I commanded you, 'You shall not eat of it,' cursed is the ground because of you; in pain you shall eat of it all the days of your life; thorns and thistles it shall bring forth for you; and you shall eat the plants of the field. By the sweat of your face you shall eat bread, till you return to the ground, for out of it you were taken; for you are dust, and to dust you shall return. (Gen. 3:17-19)

The *1689 Baptist Confession of Faith* sums up the great height from which humanity has fallen: "Our first parents, by this sin, fell from their original righteousness and communion with God, and we in them whereby death came upon all: all becoming dead in sin, and wholly defiled in all the faculties and parts of soul and body."[2] And Ephesians 2:1-3 affirms the horrific results of Adam's sin:

> And you were dead in the trespasses and sins in which you once walked, following the course of this world, following the prince of the power of the air, the spirit that is now at work in the sons of disobedience— among whom we all once lived in the passions of our flesh, carrying out the desires of the body and the mind, and were by nature children of wrath, like the rest of mankind.

God's good creation was rendered hopeless and helpless when sin entered the world (Eph. 2:12). Darkness reigned that day as the curse fell upon the face of the earth.

THE PRECURSOR TO SIN

Before the serpent tempted our first parents, another drama unfolded that has cosmic implications. Before God fashioned the cosmos, he created Lucifer. Ezekiel 28:12-19 describes him as the highest of the created beings: "You were the signet of perfection, full of wisdom and perfect in beauty" (v. 12). He was a glorious creature, created to praise God; an anointed cherub with the responsibility of serving the living God and upholding his sovereign rule and government (vv. 13-14). He was created in a blameless condition: "You were blameless in your ways from the day you were created, till unrighteousness was found in you" (v. 15). But Lucifer's pride gave rise to rebellion, and he fell into sin:

> In the abundance of your trade you were filled with violence in your midst, and you sinned; so I cast you as a profane thing from the mountain of God, and I destroyed you, O guardian cherub, from the midst of the stones of fire. Your heart was proud because of your beauty; you corrupted your wisdom for the sake of your splendor; I cast you to the ground; I exposed you before Kings, to feast their eyes on you. (Ezek. 28:16-17)

Pride, which is rooted in unbelief, fails to believe God, honor God, and find satisfaction in his all-wise promises. Pride and unbelief, then, is the root of every sinful decision and action. Daniel Fuller adds, "Therefore we should understand our total depravity to consist in heaping the greatest insult upon God by refusing to regard him as trustworthy."[3] Fuller's focus is on humanity but his reasoning applies to Lucifer's rebellion against God.

The sinful motive of Lucifer is clearly revealed in the five "I will's," of Isaiah 14, which are an expression of sinful independence and self-worship: "You said in your heart, 'I will ascend to heaven; above the stars of God I will set my throne on high; I will sit on the mount of assembly in the far reaches of the north; I will ascend above the heights of the clouds; I will make myself like the Most High'" (Isa. 14:13–14). Jonathan Edwards adds, "Satan the greatest of all mere creatures fell precisely because he would not humble himself. He was cast down to earth and hell."[4] Satan's pride and narcissism were evident in his posture before a holy God.

The fall of Satan is included in God's eternal decree, who according to Scripture predestines everything "according to the counsel of his will" (Eph. 1:11). John Piper describes the purpose of God in permitting the fall of Satan: "I conclude, therefore, that God permitted Satan's fall, not because he was unable to stop it, but because he had a purpose for it. Since God is never taken off guard, his permissions are always purposeful. If he chooses to permit something, he does so for a reason – an infinitely wise reason because he is infinitely wise."[5] Indeed, God rules over heaven and hell; his eternal decrees oversee every human decision – good or evil, and is sovereign over every demon in hell. His purposes will be accomplished, even in the midst of horrifying sin.

THE PERPLEXING OSTRICH SYNDROME

I define the Ostrich Syndrome as "the unwillingness to admit that sin or evil exists." The Ostrich Syndrome has been advocated by many people including poets, philosophers, atheists, agnostics, and even theists.

Timothy Keller reminds us how deeply biased we have become toward anything that resembles the devil: "To us, Satan is a personification of evil left over from a pre-scientific, superstitious society. He's just a symbol now, an ironic way to deflect personal responsibility for evil."[6] In a word, we are too sophisticated to believe in such a diabolical figure.

A gentleman once told me on a plane, "There is no problem with evil." Apparently, other people agree with this position. One individual posted a comment online: "Bad people do bad things. Good people do good things. Bad things happen. These things are 'wrong' and must be accounted for - but this is not evil."[7] The same individual writes, "There are Hitlers and Mansons who commit atrocities that are way beyond very wrong. In their minds the acts they were committing were necessary to accomplish a 'good' they perceived just as with slavery and other crimes against humanity and life. These things may be unspeakably wrong and bad – but they are not evil."

The founder of *Christian Science*, Mary Baker Eddy taught that evil is an illusion. Clearly, then, we find a variety of people who fall prey to the Ostrich Syndrome. Denying or minimizing sin may appear to blunt the razor-sharp edges of this massive problem, but unfortunately, it only exacerbates the problem of evil with greater severity. The ostrich can only keep her head in the ground for so long. One can temporarily ignore Hitler's Third Reich, Stalin's gulag system, the rise of atheistic Marxism, and Chairman Mao's evil reign in China – but in the end, evil inevitably raises her ugly head.

THE PERVASIVENESS OF SIN

Plagues, the holocaust, pandemics, rape, murder, suicide, birth defects, still-born babies, mental disorders, and diseases such as Alzheimer's, AIDS, cancer, ALS, and leukemia are all practical examples of the pervasive nature of evil in our world. The Bible speaks candidly about the diabolical nature of sin:

> But understand this, that in the last days there will come times of difficulty. For people will be lovers of self, lovers of money, proud, arrogant, abusive, disobedient to their parents, ungrateful, unholy, heartless, unappeasable, slanderous, without self-control, brutal, not loving good, treacherous, reckless, swollen with conceit, lovers of pleasure rather than lovers of God, having the appearance of godliness, but denying its power. Avoid such people. (2 Tim. 3:1–5)
>
> And because lawlessness will be increased, the love of many will grow cold. (Matt. 24:12)
>
> Beloved, do not be surprised at the fiery trial when it comes upon you to test you, as though something strange were happening to you. (1 Pet. 4:12)

C.S. Lewis well-understood sin and its horrifying effects:

> When I think of pain – of anxiety that gnaws like fire and loneliness that spreads out like a desert, and the heartbreaking routine of monotonous misery, or again of dull aches that blacken our whole landscape or sudden nauseating pains that knock a man's heart out at one blow, of pains that seem already intolerable and then are suddenly increased, of infuriating scorpion-stinging pains that startle into maniacal movement of a man who seemed half dead with his previous tortures ... If I knew a way of escape I would crawl through the sewers to escape the pain.[8]

Sin has not always been a part of this world, but it *has* been a part of God's eternal plan. "Sin was the origin of evil; it was not the context of the pre-fallen world."[9] Indeed, God's sovereign purposes in allowing evil serve to magnify the glory and the greatness of his grace. Apart from sin and Christ's horrifying crucifixion, there would be no path to put God's glory on full display.[10]

Sin has not always existed, but God in his sovereignty ordained that sin should be so his glory would shine with white-hot intensity! Joni Eareckson Tada rightly says, "God permits what he hates to accomplish that which he loves." That is, God has and will continue to be glorified, despite the sinful decisions that creatures make each day. There is no pointless pain in God's economy. Rather, God uses all things (even sin) to the praise of his glorious grace.

In this book, we will discover that the penalty of sin and the power of sin has been dethroned in the lives of every Christ-follower. This wonderful news is only due to the completed work of Jesus, namely, his life, death, burial, glorious resurrection, and ascension. And one day, the very presence of sin will be gone forever. But we are getting ahead of ourselves. We must first begin by learning about the nature of sin.

---

1. WCF, Chapter 6, Sec. 1.
2. Samuel E. Waldron, A Modern Exposition of the 1689 Baptist Confession of Faith (Webster: Evangelical Press, 1989), 92.
3. Daniel P. Fuller, The Unity of the Bible: Unfolding God's Plan for Humanity (Grand Rapids: Zondervan Publishing House, 1992), 194.
4. See John Gerstner, The Rational Biblical Theology of Jonathan Edwards, 2:216.
5. John Piper, Spectacular Sins (Wheaton: Crossway Books, 2008), 47.
6. Timothy Keller, King's Cross: The Story of the World in the Life of Jesus (New York: Dutton, 2011), 11.
7. www.pfunk1.com/thereisnoevil.
8. C.S. Lewis, The Problem of Pain (San Francisco: HarperCollins Publishers, 1940), 105.
9. Douglas F. Kelly, Cited in Matthew Barrett, Ed. Reformation Theology (Wheaton: Crossway Books, 2017), 292.
10. See Scott Christensen, What About Evil? (Phillipsburg: P&R Publishing, 2020).

2

The Nature of Sin

As you grow in realization of the terrifying power of Satan, you will cling closer to God, call upon Him the more fervently, and thank Him with more ardent love for the deliverance wrought through Jesus Christ, your Savior.

ABRAHAM KUYPER

THE DATE WAS JULY 8, 1741. The lanky preacher made his way into the pulpit in Enfield, Connecticut. His practice was to begin the sermon by reading the biblical text. The eyes of the congregation gazed upon the New England preacher as he read God's infallible and authoritative Word:

> *Vengeance is mine, and recompense, for the time when their foot shall slip; for the day of their calamity is at hand, and their doom comes swiftly.*

The preacher's text, Deuteronomy 32:35, threatened the judgment of God on the wicked and unbelieving Israelites, who were God's visible people, yet remained obstinate and stiff-necked, despite the many gifts of grace that God had freely bestowed upon them.

The central thought that Jonathan Edwards developed is far removed from what usually passes for preaching in the typical American church:

> There is nothing that keeps wicked men at any one moment out of hell, but the mere pleasure of God. [1]

The sermon had a powerful effect on the hearts and minds of the congregation. Iain Murray observes, "Men suddenly, and in large numbers, are made to feel the real nature and danger of sin."[2] One eyewitness named Stephen Williams commented, "Before the sermon was done, there was a great moaning and crying out throughout the whole house. What shall I do to be saved? Oh I am going to Hell. Oh what shall I do for Christ?"[3] This marks the powerful effect of Edwards' preaching on the eighteenth-century listener.

God used the bold preaching of Edwards to awaken a people who were spiritually lethargic at best or spiritually dead at worst. His passion to unfold the horror of sin and its terrible consequences helped people see that their current condition was hopeless apart from God's saving grace in Christ. His preaching unveiled a sober biblical reality: every person has violated God's law and, as a result, is subject to eternal judgment.

What compelled Jonathan Edwards to speak in such vivid terms about the judgment of God and the sinfulness of sin? What compelled him to labor over the pitiful condition of the sinful creatures who filled the pews in Enfield? Why was the New England preacher so preoccupied with sin? The answer is found in Scripture as we explore the nature of sin.

THE EXPLANATION OF TOTAL DEPRAVITY

The Puritan pastor and theologian, Thomas Goodwin, pulls the veil back and exposes sin for what it truly is: "Hence sin, it is called poison, and sinners serpents; sin is called a vomit, sinners dogs; sin the stench of graves, and they are rotten sepulchers; sin mire, sinners sows; and sin darkness, blindness, shame, nakedness, folly, madness, death, whatever is filthy, defective, ineffective, painful."[4] The reality of sin is worse than we ever imagined.

Goodwin's description of sin reminds us at the beginning of our study of the importance of defining sin in biblical categories. Our view of sin, we shall see, will have a profound effect on our theological understanding, our approach to Scripture, temptation, and the way we live the Christian life. Indeed, it will be important to have a biblical understanding of sin if we are to live the Christian life in victory, as God intends.

Paul explains in his letter to the Romans that unbelievers "exchanged the truth of God for a lie and worshiped and served the creature rather than the Creator ..." (Rom. 1:25). And whenever truth is swapped for a lie, the result is sinful behavior which is both deviant and defiant. Cornelius Plantinga Jr. describes sin in clear terms:

> Sin is missing the target; sin is choosing the wrong target. Sin is wandering from the path or rebelling against someone too strong for us or neglecting a good inheritance. Above all, at its core, sin is offense against God ... To rebel against God is to saw off the branch that supports us ... Rebellion against God and flight from God remove us from the sphere of blessing, cutting us off from our only invisible means of support.[5]

Sinners are totally depraved. The term "depravity" is often misunderstood, so an accurate definition of total depravity is essential. Edwin Palmer writes, "Total depravity means that natural man is never able to do any good that is fundamentally pleasing to God, and, in fact, does evil all the time."[6] Total depravity does not mean that sinners are as bad as they can possibly be. The term does not suggest that all sinners are equally predisposed to commit acts of murder or steal from their neighbor. The doctrine of total depravity does suggest, however, that sinners apart from grace are incapable of doing good to the glory of God. That is, sinners apart from grace are utterly incapable of pleasing God or glorifying him in any way. Unregenerate sinners may participate in activities that are deemed "good" and "virtuous." But these acts are *always* self-motivated. They may be "good" according to worldly standards, but in the end they fail to glorify God. Rather than freely glorifying God, "the unconverted sinner is imprisoned by his sin."[7] The only free will that unconverted sinners possess, then, is the freedom to sin.

The biblical support for the doctrine of total depravity is compelling. It is also overwhelming and devastating. God's warning to Adam was plain and unambiguous. We've seen how Adam and Eve were deceived by the serpent and succumbed to sin (2 Cor. 11:3). Scripture unpacks the doctrine of total depravity and leaves us humbled to the core:

> The LORD saw that the wickedness of man was great in the earth, and that every intention of the thoughts of his heart was only evil continually. (Gen. 6:5)
>
> And when the LORD smelled the pleasing aroma, the LORD said in his heart, 'I will never again curse the ground because of man, for the intention of man's heart is evil from his youth. Neither will I ever again strike down every living creature as I have done.' (Gen. 8:21)
>
> The fool has said in his heart, 'There is no God.' They are corrupt, they do abominable deeds, there is none who does good. The LORD looks

down from heaven on the children of man, to see if there are any who understand, who seek after God. They have all turned aside; together they have become corrupt; there is none who does good, not even one. (Ps. 53:1-3)

Behold, I was brought forth in iniquity, and in sin did my mother conceive me. (Ps. 51:5)

The heart is deceitful above all things, and desperately sick; who can understand it. (Jer. 17:9)

All we like sheep have gone astray; we have turned every one to his own way; and the LORD has laid on him the iniquity of us all. (Isa. 53:6)

We have all become like one who is unclean, and all our righteous deeds are like a polluted garment. We all fade like a leaf, and our iniquities, like the wind, take us away. (Isa. 64:6)

For my people are foolish; they know me not; they are stupid children; they have no understanding. They are 'wise' in doing evil! But how to do good they know not. (Jer. 4:22)

And you were dead in the trespasses and sins in which you once walked, following the course of this world, following the prince of the power of the air, the spirit that is now at work in the sons of disobedience – among whom we all once lived in the passions of our flesh, carrying out the desires of the body and the mind, and were by nature children of wrath, like the rest of mankind. (Eph. 2:1-3)

Therefore, just as sin came into the world through one man, and death through sin, and so

> death spread to all men because all sinned. (Rom. 5:12)
>
> And you, who were dead in your trespasses and the uncircumcision of your flesh, God made alive together with him, having forgiven us all our trespasses. (Col. 2:13)
>
> Jesus answered them, 'Truly, truly, I say to you, everyone who practices sin is a slave to sin.' (John 8:34)
>
> For from within, out of the heart of man, come evil thoughts, sexual immorality, theft, murder, adultery, coveting, wickedness, deceit, sensuality, envy, slander, pride, foolishness. (Mark 7:21-22)

THE EXTENT OF TOTAL DEPRAVITY

The extent of sin is tragic and far-reaching. Thomas Goodwin reveals the devastating effects of sin: "It rests not in one member only, but beginning at the understanding, eats into the will and affections, soaks through all. Those diseases we account strongest, which seize not on a joint or a member only, but strike rottenness through the whole body."[8] Paul explains the effects of sin in Romans 5:12. He writes, "Therefore, just as sin came into the world through one man, and death through sin, and so death spread to all men because all sinned." This sin created a massive chasm between the creature and the Creator. This sin separated us from a holy God. Isaiah 59:2 says, "But your iniquities have made a separation between you and your God, and your sins have hidden his face from you."

The authors of the *Westminster Confession of Faith* help us understand the tragic effects of sin upon the human race: "Every sin, both original and actual, being a transgression of the righteous law of God, and contrary thereunto, doth in its own nature, bring guilt upon the sinner, whereby he is bound over to the wrath of God, and curse of the law, and so made subject to death, with all miseries spiritual, temporal, and eternal."[9]

Notice a few helpful definitions of total depravity, i.e., total inability:

> What we mean is that the whole of human nature was ethically perverted so as to become wholly contrary to God. Thus *every part* of that which constitutes man's created nature was polluted and corrupted ... The 'total' in 'total depravity' refers to the *extent* of damage rather than the *degree.*[10]

> This doctrine of Total Inability, which declares that men are dead in sin, does not mean that all men are equally bad, nor that any man is as bad as he could be, nor that anyone is entirely destitute of virtue, nor that human nature is evil in itself, nor that man's spirit is inactive, and much less does it mean that the body is dead. What it does mean is that since the fall man rests under the curse of sin, that he is actuated by wrong principles, and that he is wholly unable to love God or to do anything meriting salvation.[11]

> That corruption whereby man is utterly indisposed, disabled, and made opposite to all that is spiritually good.[12]

> ...Man since the fall is utterly indisposed, disabled, and made opposite to all good, and wholly inclined to all evil. He possesses a fixed bias of the will against God, and instinctively and willingly turns to evil ... Man is a free agent but he cannot originate the love of God in his heart. His will is free in the sense that it is not controlled by any

> force outside himself. As the bird with a broken wing is 'free' to fly but not able, so the natural man is free to come to God but not able.[13]
>
> Sin must be understood from a theocentric or God-centered standpoint. At its core, sin is a violation of the Creator-creature relationship. Man only exists because God made him, and man is in every sense obligated to serve his Creator. Sin causes man to assume the role of God and to assert autonomy for himself apart from the Creator. The most all-encompassing view of sin's mainspring, therefore, is the demand for autonomy ... Man's spiritual state is not one of relative neutrality, in which he is able to accept or reject God and his gospel. He is an active hater of God.[14]

There is a common theme that runs through each of these definitions. Nothing is untouched in people who have been affected by the horrible grip of sin. The effects of sin have penetrated every aspect of every person – heart, mind, emotions, and will.

Al Martin observes the hideous effect of sin in stark terms: "Every stirring of envy, if it had its way, would lead to murder and destruction. Every doubt of any phrase of Scripture, if it had its way, would eat to the ultimate denial of God and of every truth of Scripture. Every breathing of pride in its first stirrings, if it had its way, would run and tear the crown off God's head."[15]

Any attitude or action that violates the Word of God or stands opposed to his authority is sin. Repudiating the truth of God is tantamount to sin. "Every sin," writes Thomas Watson, "is treason against the crown of heaven. Now, the more treasons a person commits, the more he enrages his prince. To sin still is to dare God's justice; 'tis to affront him to his face, and an affront will make God draw his sword."[16]

Scripture provides a long list of effects that plague each person. The pervasiveness of sin strikes a devastating blow on every creature:

- Sinners are born, not made (Ps. 51:5; Rom. 5:12).
- The heart is wicked, foolish, and darkened (Jer. 17:9; Rom. 1:21-22; Gen. 6:5; 8:21; Ps. 101:4).
- The heart devises wicked schemes (Prov. 6:18).
- The heart breeds evil thoughts, murder, adultery, sexual immorality, theft, false witness, and slander (Matt. 15:19; Luke 6:45).
- No righteousness (Rom. 3:10).
- No desire for God (Rom. 3:11).
- No inclination to do good for the glory of God (Rom. 3:12).
- A hatred for God and the ways of God (Rom. 8:7-8).
- Hostility to God (Rom. 8:7-8; Col. 1:21).
- No fear of God (Rom. 3:18).
- Darkened minds and futile thinking (Eph. 4:18; 1 Cor. 2:14; Rom. 1:21).
- Depraved minds (1 Tim. 6:5).
- Alienated from the life of God because of ignorance (Eph. 4:18).
- Hard-hearted (Eph. 4:18).

- Given over to sensuality, greed, and impurity (Eph. 4:19).
- Under the wrath of God apart from the saving benefits of Christ (Rom. 1:18).
- An ungodly truth suppressor (Rom. 1:18).
- Fools who engage in idolatry (Rom. 1:23-25).
- Eyes that are spiritually blind (John 3:3).
- Feet that rush to commit evil (Prov. 1:15-16; Isa. 59:2-7).
- Thoughts that are filled with iniquity (Isa 59:7).

EXPLORING THE CONTOURS OF SIN

Sin casts a dark shadow over our world, and its curse presses into our daily lives. No one is untouched by the stain of sin. There is simply no escaping its grim reality. Thomas Watson says, "Sin is not only a defection, but a pollution. It is to the soul as rust is to gold, as a stain to beauty. It makes the soul red with guilt, and black with filth."[17] Jeremiah reminds us that "the heart is deceitful above all things" (Jer. 17:9). Cornelius Plantinga Jr. reminds us about the horrific nature of sin:

> Sin is faithlessness, lawlessness, godlessness. Sin is both the overstepping of a line and the failure to reach it – both transgression and shortcoming. Sin is a missing of the mark, a spoiling of goods, a staining of garments, a hitch in one's gait, a wandering from the path, a fragmenting of the whole. Sin is what culpably *disturbs* shalom. Sinful human life is a caricature of proper human life ... Sin does not build shalom; it vandalizes it.[18]

The Bible tells us that sin is a part of the warp and woof of daily life. The pages of Scripture provide at least eight solemn reminders about sin.

First, *it reminds us about the reality of sin*. Psalm 14:3 says, "They have all turned aside; together they have become corrupt; there is none who does good, not even one." Brian Hedges paints a picture that everyone can relate to. He says, "Sin is chocolate-covered poison."[19]

Second, *it reminds us about the perverse nature of sin*. Isaiah 64:6 says, "We have all become like one who is unclean, and all our righteous deeds are like a polluted garment. We all fade like a leaf, and our iniquities, like the wind, take us away." Thomas Watson writes, "Sin is a thorn in the conscience. It is a sword in the bones. Whatever deflowers, disturbs. Yet, such is the love that a man bears to his sin that he will venture for all his lusts – the loss of God's favor and the loss of his soul."[20]

Third, *it reminds us about the enslaving effects of sin*. Jesus says, "Truly, truly, I say to you, everyone who practices sin is a slave to sin" (John 8:34). Both Scripture (Jer. 17:9; Rom. 3:23) and experience tell us that every unconverted person commits sin as a habit; therefore every unconverted person is a slave to sin. *Slave* comes from the word *doūlos*. John MacArthur describes the radical effects of sin on the unbeliever's life:

> Sin is a cruel tyrant. It is the most devastating and degenerating power ever to afflict the human race ... It corrupts the entire person – infecting the soul, polluting the mind, defiling the conscience, contaminating the affections, and poisoning the will. It is the life-destroying, soul-condemning cancer that festers and grows in every unredeemed human heart like an incurable gangrene.[21]

Scripture clearly declared the spiritual bondage that every unconverted person is under:

> In the same way we also, when we were children, were enslaved to the elementary principles of the world. (Gal. 4:3)
>
> They promise them freedom, but they themselves are slaves of corruption. For whatever overcomes a person, to that he is enslaved. (2 Pet. 2:19)

Every person remains in bondage to spiritual slavery, until the Son sets them free. The answer, of course, to spiritual slavery is found in Christ. The answer is the gospel! "So if the Son sets you free, you will be free indeed" (John 8:36).

Fourth, *the Bible reminds us that we have been born into sin.* David confesses, "Behold, I was brought forth in iniquity, and in sin did my mother conceive me" (Ps. 51:5). Ralph Venning adds, "Sin is an anti-will to God's will; it sets itself to oppose preaching, prayer, and all the institutions of God."[22]

Fifth, *the Bible reminds of debilitating effects of sin.* "For the mind that is set on the flesh is hostile to God, for it does not submit to God's law; indeed it cannot; Those who are in the flesh cannot please God" (Rom. 8:7-8).

The *hostility* that Paul refers to is deep-seated ill will and animosity that is directed at God. The same Greek term is translated as *enmity* in Galatians 5:20.[23] Jonathan Edwards addressed this hostility in his book, *Men Naturally God's Enemies:*

> Their enmity appears in their judgments, their natural relish, their wills, affections, and practice

> ... They count him worthy neither to be loved nor feared.
>
> They are enemies in the natural relish of their souls. They have an inbred distaste and disrelish for God's perfections.
>
> Their wills are contrary to his will.
>
> They are enemies to God in their affections ... the heart is like a viper, hissing and spitting poison at God.
>
> They are enemies in their practice ... They are engaged in war against God. [24]

The mind of the unbeliever does not *submit* to God's law. Slaves of sin are simply *unwilling* to submit to God. More than that, they are *unable* to submit to God. "Freewill," writes Luther, "is nothing but the slave of sin, death and Satan, not doing anything, nor able to do or attempt anything, but evil."[25] Ralph Venning adds, "Sin makes the heart hard and God's ear deaf."[26] Cornelius Plantinga Jr. says, "Self-deception about our sin is a narcotic, a tranquilizing and disorienting suppression of our spiritual central nervous system."[27] Unbelieving people lack the ability, inclination, and desire to submit to God.

Paul concludes by noting that *unbelievers cannot please God*. The author of Hebrews agrees: "And without faith it is impossible to please him, for whoever would draw near to God must believe that he exists and that he rewards those who seek him" (Heb. 11:6).

Sixth, *the Bible reminds of the horrific effects of sin*. Paul paints this devastating portrait in Ephesians 4:18-19. He says, "They are darkened in their understanding, alienated from the life of God because of the ignorance that is in them, due to their hardness of heart. They have become callous and have given themselves up to sensuality, greedy to practice every kind of impurity."

Next, *the Bible reminds us about the comprehensiveness of sin.* "For all have sinned and fall short of the glory of God (Rom. 3:23). Everyone has sinned. There are no exceptions. To sin means "to miss the mark." *The New City Catechism* explains: "Sin is rejecting or ignoring God in the world he created, rebelling against him by living without reference to him, not being or doing what he requires in his law – resulting in our death and the disintegration of all creation."[28]

Apart from grace:

- Every sinner is an enemy of God (Rom. 5:10).
- Every sinner is separated from God (Eph. 2:12).
- Every sinner is under the almighty wrath of God (John 3:36).
- Every sinner faces physical and spiritual death (Gen. 2:17; Rom. 6:23).

Additionally, all people fall short of God's glory. Instead of glorifying God, we fell dreadfully short:

- Instead of rejoicing in God, we repudiated God.
- Instead of reveling in God, we rebelled against God.
- Instead of relying on God, we ran from God.
- Instead of praising God, we profaned God.
- Instead of calling out to God, we cursed God.
- Instead of delighting in God, we despised God.

I cannot think of anything more horrifying than a creature, made in the image of God and created to glorify God, who willingly turns away from him. Daniel Fuller's remarks capture the essence of this willful mutiny:

> We should understand our total depravity primarily to consist in heaping the greatest insult upon God (emphasis mine) by refusing to regard him as trustworthy ...
>
> ... So the enormity of people's total depravity consists both in treating God in the worst possible way and deterring others from knowing the unsurpassed blessing of having him work for them to do them good with his whole heart and soul. The enormity of such a crime therefore requires a punishment having a corresponding severity ... We therefore conclude that it is just and right for God to consign the impenitent to an eternal hell.[29]

Finally, *the Bible reminds us about the penalty of sin*:

> For the wages of sin is death, but the free gift of God is eternal life in Christ Jesus our Lord. (Rom. 6:23)

Additionally, the catechisms and confessions underscore the extent of total depravity:

The New England Primer (1777)

"In Adam's Fall, we sinned all."

The Belgic Confession (1561)

"We believe that, through the disobedience of Adam, original sin is extended to all mankind; which is a corruption of the whole nature, and an hereditary disease, wherewith infants themselves are infected even in their mother's womb, and which produceth in man all sorts of sin, being in him as a root thereof; and therefore is so vile and abominable in the sight of God, that it is sufficient to condemn all mankind" (Article XV: "Original Sin).

Westminster Confession of Faith (1647)

"By this sin they fell from their original righteousness and communion with God, and so became dead in sin, and *wholly defiled* (emphasis added) in all the faculties and parts of soul and body" (Chapter 6, Sec. 2).

"From this original corruption, whereby we are utterly indisposed, disabled, and made opposite to all good, and wholly inclined to all evil, do proceed all actual transgressions" (Chapter 6, Sec. 4).

Spurgeon's Catechism (1855)

"The sinfulness of that state whereinto man fell, consists in the guilt of Adam's first sin (Rom. 5:19), the want of original righteousness (Rom. 3:10), and the corruption of his *whole nature* (emphasis added), which is commonly called original sin (Eph. 2:1; Ps. 51:5), together with all actual transgressions which proceed from it" (Matt. 15:19).

The Baptist Catechism (1689)

Our first parents, by this sin, fell from their original righteousness and communion with God, and we in them, whereby death came upon all: all becoming dead in sin, and *wholly defiled* (emphasis added) in all the faculties and parts of soul and body (Chapter 2: "Of the Fall of Man, of Sin, and of Punishment Thereof").

Sin is woven throughout the pages of Scripture and embroidered into the fabric of our lives. The New England Puritans understood and embraced the nature of sin. In the classic devotional, *The Valley of Vision*, one writer explains the horror and gravity of sin:

> Sin is my malady, my monster, my foe, my viper, born in my birth, alive in my life, strong in my character, dominating my faculties, following me as a shadow, intermingling with my every thought, my chain that holds me captive in the empire of my soul.[30]

Jonathan Edwards preached and often wrote about the nature of sin. Proclaiming the reality of sin was necessary for Edwards to be numbered among the faithful. He labored to unpack this weighty doctrine to his congregation, which would ultimately drive them to seek grace and forgiveness from God through Jesus Christ. But not everyone accepts the biblical reality of sin, as we shall see in the next chapter.

---

1. The Works of Jonathan Edwards, Sinners in the Hands of an Angry God, ed. Edward Hickman (Edinburgh: Banner of Truth, reprint 1992), 2:7.
2. Iain Murray, Jonathan Edwards: A New Biography (Edinburgh: Banner of Truth, 1987), 169.
3. Stephen Williams, Cited in George M. Marsden, Jonathan Edwards: A Life (New Haven: Yale University Press, 2003), 220.

4. "Aggravation of Sin," in The Works of Thomas Goodwin, (Grand Rapids: Soli Deo Gloria Publications reprint 2021), 4:155.
5. Cornelius Plantinga Jr. Not the Way It's Supposed to Be: A Breviary of Sin (Grand Rapids: Eerdmans Publishing Company, 1995), 123-124.
6. Edwin H. Palmer, The Five Points of Calvinism (Grand Rapids: Baker Books, 1972), 13.
7. Steven J. Lawson, Foundations of Grace (Lake Mary: Reformation Trust, 2006), 1:347.
8. Thomas Goodwin, "Aggravation of Sin," in The Works of Thomas Goodwin, 4:154.
9. G.I. Williamson, Ed. The Westminster Confession of Faith (Philadelphia: P&R, 1964), 77.
10. Ibid., 72.
11. Loraine Boettner, The Reformed Doctrine of Predestination (Philadelphia: P&R, 1969), 61.
12. Westminster Larger Catechism, 25. Cited in G.T. Shedd, Dogmatic Theology (Phillipsburg: P&R, 2003), 577.
13. Loraine Boettner, The Reformed Doctrine of Predestination, 62.
14. John MacArthur and Richard Mayhue, Biblical Doctrine: A Systematic Summary of Bible Truth (Wheaton: Crossway Books, 2017), 453.
15. Al Martin, "Practical Helps to Mortification of Sin," Banner of Truth, 30. Cited in Wayne Mack A Fight to the Death: Taking Aim at Sin Within (Phillipsburg: P&R, 2006), 37.
16. Thomas Watson, The Mischief of Sin (Pittsburgh: Soli Deo Gloria Publications, 1994), 63.
17. Thomas Watson, A Body of Divinity (Edinburgh: Banner of Truth, 1692), 133.
18. Cornelius Plantinga Jr., Not the Way It's Supposed to Be: A Breviary of Sin, 88-89.
19. Brian G. Hedges, Licensed to Kill: A Field Manual for Mortifying Sin (Adelphi: Cruciform Press, 2011), 2011.

20. Watson, The Mischief of Sin, 56.
21. John F. MacArthur, Slave (Nashville: Thomas Nelson, 2010), 120-121.
22. Ralph Venning, The Sinfulness of Sin, Loc. 136.
23. We also see this word in James 4:4: "You adulterous people! Do you not know that friendship with the world is enmity with God? Therefore whoever wishes to be a friend of the world makes himself an enemy of God" (Jas. 4:4).
24. Jonathan Edwards, "Men Naturally God's Enemies," in The Works of Jonathan Edwards, 2:130-131.
25. Martin Luther, The Bondage of the Will (Westwood: Revel Company, reprint 1957), 301.
26. Venning, The Sinfulness of Sin, Loc. 58.
27. Cornelius Plantinga Jr., Not the Way It's Supposed to Be: A Breviary of Sin, xiii.
28. The New City Catechism (Wheaton: Crossway Books, 2017), 47.
29. Daniel Fuller, The Unity of the Bible (Grand Rapids: Zondervan, 1992), 194.
30. Arthur Bennett, Ed. The Valley of Vision: A Collection of Puritan Prayers and Devotions (Edinburgh: Banner of Truth, 1975), 75.

3

THE REPUDIATION OF SIN

Oh, let not the devil succeed in persuading you that sin is a small matter!

J.C. RYLE

I'LL NEVER FORGET THE day my wife brought our daughter into this world. She was absolutely beautiful (and still is!). Everyone in the room was stunned by this wonderful new baby. "She's perfect in every way," someone in the room observed. My insensitive reply broke the mood when I personalized Psalm 51:5, "She may be beautiful, but she was still born in sin."

The last thing anyone wants to hear is that their sweet child is a sinner. I recently received an email from a gentleman who took it one step further. "Each person is born in a state of innocence," he said. Knowingly or unknowingly, he was merely parroting the ideas of John Locke who maintained that humans are born *tabula rasa*, that is, each person, according to Locke, is born with a "blank slate." Locke intended to communicate the notion that the identity of people is completely shaped by the events after their birth. In other words, people may be affected negatively by a decadent culture, and the ideology of the world system, but in effect remain innocent until they make a choice to move in a sinful direction.

THE EXTINCTION OF TOTAL DEPRAVITY

We have learned about the origin of sin and the nature of sin. We have witnessed the tragic effects of sin on our world and in our personal lives. Despite the overwhelming evidence of total depravity, this doctrine has its detractors, both in church history and in our day as well. In this chapter, we will survey the thinking of three individuals who have undercut this important doctrine. Two of these individuals are no longer with us. The other individual is a contemporary writer who has a significant influence on many people, especially people in the church. Instead of being faithful to the Bible, these thinkers redefine total depravity or would just as soon see the doctrine rendered extinct.

Pelagius

We begin with Pelagius, who is the most serious offender. Pelagius was a British monk (354-420 A.D.) who believed that people could attain salvation through their own free efforts, apart from grace. He was marked out as a heretic at the ecumenical council in Ephesus (A.D. 431) and left a godless legacy for generations. R.C Sproul summarizes he tenants of Pelagianism capture the heart of this God-dishonoring worldview:[1]

- He denied that human sin is inherited from Adam and that death is the penalty for Adam's sin.
- He taught that God predestines no one, except in the sense that he foresees who will believe and who will reject his gracious influences.
- He argued strenuously for free will, which is the cornerstone of Pelagianism.

Alistair McGrath summarizes the essence of the Pelagian worldview:

> Pelagius taught that the resources of salvation are located within humanity. Individual human beings have the capacity to save themselves. They are not trapped by sin, but have the ability to do all that is necessary to be saved. Salvation is something which is earned through good works, which place God under an obligation to humanity. Pelagius marginalizes the idea of grace, understanding it in terms of demands made of humanity by God in order that salvation may be achieved – such as the Ten Commandments or the moral example of Christ. The ethos of Pelagianism could be summed up as 'salvation by merit,' whereas Augustine taught salvation by grace.[2]

For Pelagius, the command in Scripture to obey implies an implicit ability to obey. When the will is properly engaged, argues Pelagius, virtue is the result. This virtue is the supreme good and is followed by reward. By his own effort, man can achieve whatever is required of him in religion and morality. For Pelagius, then, it would be inconsistent and unjust for God to give a command that the creature could not obey. Making such a command without giving creatures the ability to obey would be tantamount to unfairness, according to Pelagius.

Against Locke and Pelagius, the apologist Athanasius (296-373 A.D.) held that after the Fall, people were not only born into sin and corrupted by it, but this sin also grew exponentially:

> Indeed, they had in their sinning surpassed all limits; for, having invented wickedness in the beginning and so involved themselves in death and corruption, they had gone on gradually from bad to worse, not stopping at any one kind of evil, but

> continually, as with insatiable appetite, devising new kinds of sins. [3]

Much to the chagrin of Locke and Pelagius, Scripture clearly teaches that every person is a sinner - by nature and choice.

The Heidelberg Catechism argues that sinners are born, not made. Notice Question 7: "Then where does this corrupt human nature come from?" Answer: "From the fall and disobedience of our first parents, Adam and Eve, in Paradise. This fall has so poisoned our nature that we are born sinners - corrupt from conception on."[4]

Whenever sin is minimized or marginalized, we "pay tribute" to the Pelagian lie. Whenever the "free will" of the creature is exalted, we honor the Pelagian heresy. Whenever the sinner is granted the built-in right and ability to believe the gospel apart from God's empowerment and grace, we dishonor God and the gospel of his Son. Simply put, Pelagianism is alive and well. This malicious heresy has and always will deceive and destroy people. It makes promises, but it always fails to deliver. Pelagianism, in the final analysis, celebrates the abilities of the creature and fails to honor the Creator (Rom. 1:22-23). As such, this devious theological system will continue to hinder the progress and momentum in the church. But Pelagius was not the only one to compromise the doctrine of sin.

Charles Finney

Charles Finney helped continue the tragic legacy of Pelagius by advancing his unbiblical views concerning total depravity. A trained lawyer, Finney was later ordained as a Presbyterian. But as Phillip Johnson points out, Finney received his ordination papers under false pretenses as he "disagreed on almost every point" of the *Westminster Confession*, the document that he professed allegiance to in his ordination.[5] Johnson adds, "... He accepted the platform he had duped those men into giving him—then used it for the rest of his life to attack their doctrinal convictions."[6]

Finney's repudiation of original sin is clear and unambiguous. First, *he held to an unfettered will*. Finney believed that sinners have the ability to obey God apart from grace. Listen how he dogmatically elevates the fallen will of the creature: "The moral government of God everywhere assumes and implies the liberty of the human will, and the natural ability of men to obey God. Every command, every threatening, every expostulation and denunciation in the Bible implies and assumes this."[7] Such thinking has spread like wildfire in the local church and continues to decimate the Christian mind and lead the unsuspecting down a God-dishonoring path.

The unfettered will serves as the cornerstone of Finney's worldview: "The human mind necessarily assumes the freedom of the human will as a first truth."[8] Finney beat the drum of libertarian free will with reckless abandon:

> In all our judgments respecting our own moral character and that of others, we always and necessarily assume the liberty of the human will, or natural ability to obey God.[9]
>
> ... and I know, too, that with all their theorizing, they did assume, in common with all other men, that man is free in the sense that he has liberty or power to will as God commands.[10]
>
> But the fact is, that in all cases the assumption has lain deep in the mind as a first truth, that men are free in the sense of being naturally able to obey God: and this assumption is a necessary condition of the affirmation that moral character belongs to man.[11]

Second, *he rejected the distinction between natural and moral inability.* Finney responds directly to Jonathan Edwards, who maintained a distinction between natural inability and moral inability. Edwards rejected the notion of self-determination and affirmed the total inability of sinners to render obedience to God. These views set Finney on edge and led to sharp stabs of rebuke. Finney charged Edwards with "fatalism" and marveled at what he conceived as "nonsensical." Listen to Finney's response to Jonathan Edwards:

> It is amazing to see how so great and good a man could involve himself in a metaphysical fog, and bewilder himself and his readers to such a degree, that an absolutely senseless distinction should pass into the current phraseology, philosophy, and theology of the church, and a score of theological dogmas be built upon the assumption of its truth. This nonsensical distinction has been in the mouth of the Edwardsean school of theologians, from Edwards's day to the present.[12]
>
> We have ability to obey the direct command directly, and the indirect command indirectly. That is, we are able by virtue of our nature, together with the proffered grace of the Holy Spirit, to comply with all the requirements of God. So that in fact there is no proper inability about it.[13]

Third, *he is driven more by human reason than divine revelation.* That sinners have the ability or capacity to obey God apart from gracious influences is seen as a "first truth" by Finney:

> We have seen that the *ability* (emphasis mine) of all men of sane mind to obey God, is necessarily assumed as a first truth, and that this assump-

> tion is from the very laws of mind, the indispensable condition of the affirmation, or even the conception, that they are subjects of moral obligation; that, but for this assumption, men could not so much conceive the possibility of moral responsibility, and of praiseworthiness and blameworthiness ... If the laws of mind remain unaltered, this is and always will be so. In the eternal world and in hell, men and devils must necessarily assume their own freedom or ability to obey God, as the condition of their obligation to do so, and, consequently of their being capable of sin or holiness. Since revelation informs us that men and devils continue to sin in hell, we know that there also it must be assumed as a first truth of reason, that they are free agents, or that they have the natural ability to obey God.[14]

W.M. Paul Young

W.M. Paul Young is the well-known author of the best-selling book, *The Shack*. Critics of *The Shack* were quick to point out Young's unorthodox doctrines. For instance, the god of *The Shack* has no room for judgment or wrath. Papa confesses, "There is a lot to be mad about in the mess my kids have made and in the mess they're in. I don't like a lot of choices they make, but that anger – especially for me – is an expression of love all the same. I love the ones I am angry with just as much as those I'm not."[15] Worse yet, Papa admits to Mack, "I am not who you think I am Mackenzie. I don't need to punish people for sin. Sin is its own punishment, devouring you from the inside. It's not my purpose to punish it; it's my joy to cure it!"[16]

Any conception of God that chooses to overlook sin is tantamount to undercutting and destroying the biblical gospel. Contrary to the god of *The Shack*, wrath is referred to almost six hundred times in the Old Testament.[17] In the New Testament, the Greek word for wrath is translated as "anger, vengeance, or indignation." The term means "anger exhibited in punishment." Tozer writes, "The wrath of God is his eternal detestation of all unrighteousness ... It is the holiness of God stirred into activity against sin. It is the moving cause of that just sentence which he passes upon evildoers. God is angry against sin because sin is rebelling against his authority, a wrong done to his inviolable sovereignty."[18] John Stott speaks of God's wrath as "his steady, unrelenting, unremitting, uncompromising antagonism to evil in all its forms and manifestations."[19]

Supporters of *The Shack* were quick to defend Young and argued that his fictional book was never intended to be theological in nature. However, with the recent publication of Young's book, *Lies We Believe About God*, he takes great liberty with the doctrine of total depravity. Young acknowledges a belief in sin; however, it is redefined. Young writes, "Blind, not depraved, is our condition."[20] He continues, "Sin, then, is anything that negates or diminishes or misrepresents the truth of who you are, no matter how pretty or ugly that is."[21] Such a view finds no biblical support and is a foreign concept in Christian theology.

Young admits that sin involves "missing the mark." But he adds, "The mark is not perfect moral behavior. The 'mark' is the Truth of your being."[22] But Young goes one step further in his redefinition of sin: "And what does the truth of your being look like? God. You are made in the image of God, and the truth of your being looks like God."[23]

With Young's retooled definition of sin, he is in a position to pose an additional question: Does sin separate us from God? Young argues that the notion of sinners being separated from God is a lie: "A lot of 'my people' will believe that the following statement is in the Bible, but it isn't: 'You have sinned, and you are separated from God.'"[24] The biblical proof he offers is Romans 8:38-39, that is, "nothing can separate us from the love of God." Such an explanation, however, fails to consider the context of Romans 8, which is a clear promise to the elect of God, not the entirety of the human race.

Young's view of sin deserves at least two responses: First, *his reformulation of sin is inadequate, as the Bible clearly teaches that all people are sinners by nature and choice.* John MacArthur sheds light on the real meaning of sin:

> Sin must be understood from a theocentric or God-centered standpoint. At its core, sin is a violation of the Creator-creature relationship. Man only exists because God made him, and man is in every sense obligated to serve his Creator. Sin causes man to assume the role of God and to assert autonomy for himself apart from the Creator. The most all-encompassing view of sin's mainspring, therefore, is the demand for autonomy.[25]

When sin is redefined from a man-centered viewpoint, this only strengthens the resolve of his quest for autonomy. Yet, this is precisely what we find in Young's redefined version of sin – a Creator catering to the needs of the creature, which satisfies the creature's own autonomous bent.

However, the Scriptures paint a portrait of sinful creatures which is undeniable and devastating: "The Lord saw that the wickedness of man was great in the earth, and that every intention of the thoughts of his heart was only evil continually." (Gen. 6:5) Indeed, "The heart is deceitful above all things, and desperately sick; who can understand it?" (Jer. 17:9) Edwin Palmer writes, "Total depravity means that natural man is never able to do any good that is fundamentally pleasing to God, and, in fact, does evil all the time."[26] The biblical evidence for total depravity is overwhelming and conclusive (Ps. 51:5; Isa. 53:6; 64:6; Eph. 2:1-3; Rom. 3:23; 5:12).

Second, *the Bible clearly teaches that sinners are separated from God.* Apart from grace, sinners are without hope and are utterly cut off and separated from God. Isaiah 59:2 says, "But your iniquities have made a separation between you and your God, and your sins have hidden his face from you so that he does not hear." In his letter to the Ephesians, Paul demonstrates that sinners are separated from Christ. He refers to them as "having no hope and without God in the world" (Eph. 2:12). Our only hope, then, is found in Christ alone, who came to forgive us and reconcile us to a holy God (Eph. 2:13-22).

Like the previous influential writers, W.M. Paul Young's view of sin fails the biblical test. His view dishonors God, leads people astray, and fails to serve them in any productive way.

Anyone can oppose sin or even repudiate its very presence. But the simple fact is that sin is serious. Sin is deadly. Isaac Ambrose says, "All sins, however little they may appear to us, are against the great and holy God ... Every sin is a soul-killing poison."[27]

The hymn writer, Robert Robinson, captured the inner turmoil which is found in the heart of every Christian:

> Oh, to grace how great a debtor, daily I'm constrained to be! Let thy goodness, like a fetter, bind my wandering heart to thee: Prone to wander, Lord, I feel it, prone to leave the God I love; Here's my heart, O take and seal it; Seal it for thy courts above. [28]

Jonathan Edwards observes:

> We should be much concerned to know whether we do not live in some way of sin, because we are exceedingly prone to walk in some such way. The heart of man is naturally prone to sin; the weight of the soul is naturally that way, as the stone by its weight tendeth downwards. And there is very much of a remaining proneness to sin in the saints. Though sin be mortified in them, yet there is a body of sin and death remaining; there are all manner of lusts and corrupt inclinations. We are exceeding apt to get into some ill path or other. Man is so prone to sinful ways, that without maintaining a constant strict watch over himself, no other can be expected than that he will walk in some way of sin.[29]

Herein lies the pathology of sin: Every person is a sinner by nature and by choice. Edwards is concerned to show how followers of Jesus fight indwelling sin. While the fight will continue until we reach the Celestial City, the path to that city is filled with temptations and a host of deceptions. While sin persists in the hearts of all people, God has given his people spiritual armor that protects us in our fight against sin. That is where we turn our attention in part two, namely - *the powerful safeguard in our fight against sin*.

---

1. R.C. Sproul, Willing to Believe: The Controversy Over Free Will (Grand Rapids: Baker Books, 1997), 33-41.
2. Alistair McGrath, Reformation Thought: An Introduction (Oxford: Blackwell, 1988), 74.
3. Athanasius, On the Incarnation (The Fig Classic Series, June 2012), 14.
4. Cited in Kevin DeYoung, The Good News We Almost Forgot: Rediscovering the Gospel in a 16th Century Catechism (Chicago: Moody Publishers, 2010), 28.

5. See Phillip Johnson, A Wolf in Sheep's Clothing: How Charles Finney's Theology Ravaged the Evangelical Movement, 1998.
6. Ibid.
7. Charles G. Finney, Lectures on Systematic Theology (Whittier: Colporter Kemp, 1944 reprint), 325.
8. Ibid.
9. Ibid., 326.
10. Ibid.
11. Ibid., 326-327.
12. Ibid., 333.
13. Ibid., 340-341.
14. Ibid., 345.
15. William P. Young, The Shack (Newbury Park: Windblown Media, 2007), 119.
16. Ibid., 120.
17. Walter Elwell, Ed. Evangelical Dictionary of Theology, 888.
18. A.W. Tozer, The Attributes of God (Grand Rapids: Baker Book House, 1975), 83.
19. John R.W. Stott, The Cross of Christ (Downers Grove: InterVarsity Press, 1986), 173.
20. WM. Paul Young, Lies We Believe About God (New York: Atria Books, 2017), Loc. 296.
21. Ibid., Loc. 1645.
22. Ibid., Loc. 1643.
23. Ibid., Loc. 1645.
24. Ibid., Loc. 1663.
25. John MacArthur and Richard Mayhue, Biblical Doctrine: A Systematic Summary of Bible Truth (Wheaton: Crossway Books, 2017), 453.
26. Edwin H. Palmer, The Five Points of Calvinism (Grand Rapids: Baker Books, 1972), 13.

27. Isaac Ambrose, The Christian Warrior Wrestling with Sin, Satan, the World, and the Flesh, Loc. 596.
28. Robert Robinson, Come Thou Fount of Every Blessing.
29. "Christian Cautions; or, The Necessity of Self-Examination," in The Works of Jonathan Edwards, ed. Hickman, 2:175.

PART II: THE POWERFUL SAFEGUARD IN OUR BATTLE AGAINST SIN

We have witnessed the pathology of sin and uncovered some ways this vicious monster invades our lives. Part two explores the powerful safeguard in our battle against sin. "As you grow in realization of the terrifying power of Satan, you will cling closer to God, call upon Him the more fervently, and thank Him with more ardent love for the deliverance wrought through Jesus Christ, your Savior."[1] Our only hope is found in the shed blood of Jesus Christ on the cross and his victorious resurrection from the dead.

God calls his people to stand guard; to be battle-ready. Abraham Kuyper helps us understand the importance of standing our ground in the fight against sin: "For when we realize that Satan is busy and at his tricks, then we are on our guard; then we seek refuge in Him who has crushed Satan's head; then we close our hearts to the stealthy, murderous enemy."[2] This posture of readiness requires us to wear the full armor of God – the belt of truth, the breastplate of righteousness, the shoes of the gospel of peace, the shield of faith, and the helmet of salvation. We must wield the sword of the Spirit and pray at all times in the Spirit.

The battle rages around us. Satan tempts us, the world seduces us, and the flesh seeks to lure us in with compelling force. But the Lord, in his kindness provides a powerful safeguard in our fight against sin. It is this that we turn our attention to next.

---

1. Abraham Kuyper, The Practice of Godliness (Grand Rapids: Eerdmans Publishing Company, 1948), 20.
2. Ibid., 21.

4

Battle-Ready

The Christian approach to sin is a combination of contrition and combat.

JOEL R. BEEKE

Paul makes it plain that every Christian is in a spiritual battle. This is no ordinary battle. This is an epic spiritual war. Ephesians 6:11-12 says, "Put on the whole armor of God, that you may be able to stand against the schemes of the devil. For we do not wrestle against flesh and blood, but against the rulers, against the authorities, against the cosmic powers over this present darkness, against the spiritual forces of evil in the heavenly places." With the battlefield in plain view, we must pay close attention to the needs of a battle-ready soldier.

WE NEED THE COURAGE OF CHRIST

This is one of the pressing needs in the contemporary church. The church in our generation has grown weak-kneed and fearful. She has succumbed to the sin of passivity. The church in our day has lost its nerve. It lacks theological depth. It is missing a theological backbone.

The twenty-first-century church also lacks conviction. The fiery faith of the Puritans has all but been extinguished. The bold resolve of the Reformers has eroded. The church is spineless. Phillip Graham Ryken addresses the apostasy of Israel and poses a sobering question: "What verdict would God render about the contemporary church? The dominant sin of Jerusalem – forgetting God – has become a predominant sin in the American church."[1]

We have failed to remember that we are in an epic battle. And we have capitulated to the culture. We have lost our influence. The current state of the church reminds us of the importance of Paul's words in Ephesians 6: "Finally, be strong in the Lord and in the strength of his might" (v. 10). "With these words, Paul points Christians to the divine power operating in the risen Lord Jesus Christ.[2]

It is a command

The term *strong* in Ephesians 6:10 comes from the Greek word, *èndunamoũsthe*. It means "to be rendered capable for a task." In this instance, Paul is referring to divine capability or spiritual strength on the battlefield. That is, we are commanded to be strong and courageous in the Christian life. We are commanded to demonstrate courage on the battlefield.

The command to exert courage on the battlefield is found throughout the pages of Scripture:

> Only be strong and very courageous, being careful to do according to all the law that Moses my servant commanded you. Do not turn from it to the right hand or to the left, that you may have good success wherever you go. (Josh 1:7)

> Be of good courage, and let us be courageous for our people, and for the cities of our God, and may the LORD do what seems good to him. (2 Sam. 10:12)

> Wait for the LORD; be strong, and let your heart take courage; wait for the LORD! (Ps. 27:14)
>
> Be strong, and let your heart take courage, all you who wait for the LORD!" (Ps. 31:24)

It is centered on Jesus Christ

The command to *be strong* is a plea for spiritual courage, which is grounded in the person and work of the Lord Jesus Christ. Apart from Christ, we are weak and frail. Without him, we can do nothing (John 15:5).

The apostle Paul found his strength in Christ. He writes, "I can do all things through him who strengthens me" (Phil. 4:13). And he encourages Timothy to do the same: "You then, my child, be strengthened by the grace that is in Christ Jesus" (2 Tim. 2:1). Additionally, Paul acknowledges that the Lord gave him the strength to both proclaim the gospel and persevere in seasons of difficulty. "But the Lord stood by me and strengthened me, so that through me the message mighty be fully proclaimed and all the Gentiles might hear it. So I was rescued from the lion's mouth" (2 Tim. 4:17).

The command to *be strong* in the Lord means that we trust Jesus; we trust in his strength; we trust in his might:

> Israel saw the great power that the LORD used against the Egyptians, so the people feared the LORD, and they believed in the LORD and in his servant Moses. (Exod. 14:31)
>
> Your right hand, O LORD, glorious in power, your right hand, O LORD, shatters the enemy. (Exod.15:6)

> Yours, O LORD, is the greatness and the power and the glory and the victory and the majesty, for all that is in the heavens and in the earth is yours. Yours is the kingdom, O LORD, and you are exalted as head above all. Both riches and honor come from you, and you rule over all. In your hand are power and might, and in your hand it is to make great and to give strength to all. (1 Chron. 29:11–12)

It is counterintuitive

Finally, the courage of Christ is counterintuitive. Conventional wisdom tells us to "go it alone." Sinners are by definition independent creatures. As a result:

- We find "strength" in our wisdom.
- We find "strength" in our abilities.
- We find "strength" in our intellect.
- We find "strength" in our ingenuity.
- We find "strength" in our flesh.

Yet, all along, the Bible commands us, "*Be strong in the Lord and in the strength of his might.*" Indeed, resting in the Lord's strength is counterintuitive.

One of the greatest needs of a battle-ready soldier is the courage of Christ. One of the best ways to build the courage of Christ into your life is by being a man or woman of the Word.

- You need to read the Word of God.
- You need to study the Word of God.

- You need to memorize the Word of God.
- You need to meditate on the Word of God.
- You need to saturate your mind in the Word of God.

Do you rest in Christ's courage, or do you try to muster it up on your own? When you learn about the God who parted the Red Sea, rescued Israel from Pharaoh, delivered Shadrach, Meschach and Abednego from the fiery furnace, and raised Jesus from the dead – why would you trust anything less than the Lord? (Prov. 14:12; Jas. 4:6).

In order for you to be battle-ready, you need the courage of Christ. You need to "*be strong in the Lord and in the strength of his might*" (Eph. 6:10). When the world mocks you because you embrace absolute truth, you need the courage of Christ. When the world shuns you because they learn that you adhere to the Christian worldview, you need the courage of Christ. When you receive that scary diagnosis at the doctor's office, you need the courage of Christ. When faced with a decision whether to compromise your Christian commitment, you need the courage of Christ. When your marriage is in trouble, you need the courage of Christ. When you are betrayed, you need the courage of Christ. When you are falsely slandered, you need the courage of Christ. When you are faced with wave after wave of depression or anxiety, you need the courage of Christ. When the enemy fires his arrows of temptation in your direction, you need the courage of Christ. When you are overwhelmed with life, you need the courage of Christ.

WE NEED TO PUT ON THE ARMOR OF CHRIST

The Word of God gives us clear marching orders:

> Put on the whole armor of God, that you may be able to stand against the schemes of the devil.

> For we do not wrestle against flesh and blood, but against the rulers, against the authorities, against the cosmic powers over this present darkness, against the spiritual forces of evil in the heavenly places. Therefore take up the whole armor of God, that you may be able to withstand in the evil day, and having done all, to stand firm. (Eph. 6:11–13)

It is a command

First, Scripture commands us to "put on the whole armor of God." The armor is described in Ephesians 6:14-17 and includes the belt of truth, breastplate of righteousness, shoes of the gospel of peace, shield of faith, helmet of salvation, and the sword of the Spirit.

Putting on the armor of God is an act of the will. It involves an active participation. Also, putting on the armor of God is an act of faith. We consciously choose to obey God's Word by wearing the full armor of God.

It is constructive

Second, wearing the whole armor of God is constructive. The armor enables us to stand against the schemes of the devil. The schemes (*methodeias*) of the devil are his deceptive tactics designed to lure us away from God, the Word of God, and the people of God.[3]

The Bible says the devil disguises himself as an angel of light (2 Cor. 11:14). He is a murderer and is the father of lies (John 8:44). He is a thief who comes to steal, kill, and destroy (John 10:10). And he is the great deceiver (Rev. 12:9).

- The devil has been deceiving people from the beginning (Gen. 3:1-5).
- The devil distorts the truth.

- The devil works overtime to instill doubt in people.
- The devil works hard at discouraging people.

It is no secret that Martin Luther was one of the most important and influential leaders in the history of the church. What many people are unaware of is this: Luther battled depression for most of his adult life. In 1527, he penned these sobering words: "For more than a week, I was close to the gates of hell."[4]

The devil is on a seek and destroy mission. His aim is to annihilate the people of God. But God's Word assures us that our destiny is secure in Christ. Jesus told Peter, "And I tell you, you are Peter, and on this rock I will build my church, and the gates of hell shall not prevail against it" (Matt. 16:18). So, the command to put on the whole armor of God is constructive. It enables us to stand against the schemes of the devil.

It is calculated

Paul describes the battlefield in plain terms: "For we do not wrestle against flesh and blood, but against the rulers, against the authorities, against the cosmic powers over this present darkness, against the spiritual forces of evil in the heavenly places" (Eph. 6:12). *Wrestle* (*pálei*) is "the act of engaging in hand-to-hand combat." Paul tells us that we are in a serious battle. Yet, he reminds us that our battle is not against "flesh and blood." In other words, our battle is not against a physical foe. Our struggle is in the spiritual arena. Our struggle is against:

- Rulers (*árchás*): "any supernatural being (other than God) acting in a ruling or commanding capacity, either good or evil."
- Authorities (*éxousías*): "a person who exercises control over others."
- Cosmic powers (*kosmokrátoras*): "supernatural powers; the godless worldly system."

- Spiritual forces of evil (*poneirias*) in heavenly places.

Our struggle on the battlefield, then, is with the forces of evil that oppose God, the Word of God, and the gospel of Jesus Christ (worldly philosophy, worldviews that are opposed to God and his Word, ideologies that militate against the historic Christian faith, etc.). Never forget that our struggle is supernatural in scope. We fight in vain if we choose to fight in our own strength.

Paul tells us that we are granted supernatural ability (*duneitheitei*) to withstand the forces of darkness and stand firm. That leads us to the third great need of battle-ready soldiers (v. 13).

WE NEED TO STAND STRONG FOR CHRIST

Ephesians 6:14 instructs us to *stand*. In his landmark work on spiritual warfare, the Puritan writer William Gurnall reminds us how important it is to obey the imperative, "to stand." He writes:

> To stand is the opposite of to flee or to surrender. A captain who sees his men retreating or on the verge of surrender gives the order, 'Stand!' and every soldier worthy of his calling responds at once to his captain's voice. In like manner, every Christian is to respond to God's call to 'Stand!' — or, in other words, steadfastly to resist and never yield to the attacks of Satan.[5]

Stand means "to face or withstand something or someone with courage." "The goal of the devil," writes Ray Stedman, "is always to produce discouragement, confusion, or indifference. Whenever we find ourselves victims of a state of confusion and uncertainty, or discouragement and defeat, or an indifferent and callous attitude toward life and others, we have already become prey to the wiles of the devil."[6]

Our battle is *not* against a political party. Our battle is *not* against the government. Our battle is *not* against big tech. Our battle is *not* against any one individual or individuals. Paul states emphatically: "For we do not wrestle against flesh and blood, but against the rulers, against the authorities, against the cosmic powers over this present darkness, against the spiritual forces of evil in the heavenly places" (Eph. 6:12).

We stand against:

- *An ungodly world*. Paul warns us about the *kósmos* in his letter to the believers in Colossae: "See to it that no one takes you captive by philosophy and empty deceit, according to human tradition, according to the elemental spirits of the world, and not according to Christ" (Col. 2:8).

- *An ungodly agenda*. Scripture describes the essence of this agenda in 2 Timothy 3:1-5. "But understand this, that in the last days there will come times of difficulty. For people will be lovers of self, lovers of money, proud, arrogant, abusive, disobedient to their parents, ungrateful, unholy, heartless, unappeasable, slanderous, without self-control, brutal, not loving good, treacherous, reckless, swollen with conceit, lovers of pleasure rather than lovers of God, having the appearance of godliness, but denying its power. Avoid such people."

- *An ungodly enemy*. His name is Satan and he is backed by a hoard of evil demons. They are Satanic ambassadors who do the bidding of the prince of darkness. They seek to hinder the work of the ministry (1 Thess. 2:18). They work with all their might to stir up pride among the people of God. Ultimately, their aim is to destroy (John 10:10; Luke 22:31).

It is in the face of this kind of Satanic attack and opposition that we are called to *stand*. Such a posture is a commandment. The commandment to stand is a settled resolution. It is a mindset. In other words, before we enter the battlefield, we must embrace this settled resolution; we must establish this as a commitment; we must be energized by this mindset. We must stand!

IMPLICATIONS

Standing signifies seriousness. The Christian life is serious business. We are engaged in a war. Therefore, we must stand. Standing signifies steadfastness.

> Now I would remind you, brothers, of the gospel I preached to you, which you received, in which you stand ... (1 Cor. 15:1)
>
> Not that we lord it over your faith, but we work with you for your joy, for you stand firm in your faith. (2 Cor. 1:24)

Standing signifies spiritual strength. Paul tells his protégé, "You then, my child, be strengthened by the grace that is in Christ Jesus" (2 Tim. 2:1). *Standing signifies conviction.* It reveals our heart-felt desire to faithfully adhere to the Scripture. *Standing signifies maturity.* "Continue steadfastly in prayer, being watchful in it with thanksgiving" (Col. 4:2). Finally, *standing signifies hope.* Paul writes, "Therefore, since we have been justified by faith, we have peace with God through our Lord Jesus Christ" (Rom. 5:1).

It is time for followers of Christ to wake up and rise up! There is a battle. This battle is intense. This battle is spiritual. The great need for Christians everywhere is to be battle-ready soldiers.

1. We need the courage of Christ.

2. We need to put on the armor of Christ.

3. We need to stand strong for Christ.

The former bishop of Liverpool, J.C. Ryle warns, "Take away the gospel from a church and that church is not worth preserving. A well without water, a scabbard without a sword, a steam-engine without a fire, a ship without compass and rudder, a watch without a mainspring, a stuffed carcass without life, all these are useless things. But there is nothing so useless as a church without the gospel."[7]

Now with the bold resolve of a battle-ready soldier, we are in a position to be outfitted with the armor of God.

---

1. Phillip Graham Ryken, Courage to Stand: Jeremiah's Message for Post-Christian Times (Phillipsburg: P&R, 1998), 25.
2. Ibid., 471.
3. Methodeias is translated as "a deceptive way." The term means "craftiness, scheming, or wiles."
4. Roland Bainton, Here I Stand (New York: New American Library, n.d.), 282.
5. William Gurnall, The Christian in Complete Armour (Edinburgh: Banner of Truth, 1665), 285.

6. Ray Stedman, Spiritual Warfare (Portland: Multnomah Press, 1975), 71.
7. J.C. Ryle, Light from Old Times (Edinburgh: Banner of Truth, 2015), 45.

5

The Belt of Truth

The solider is summoned to a life of active duty and so is the Christian.

WILLIAM GURNALL

In order to stand firm and withstand the wiles of the enemy, we must put on the whole armor of God.

> Put on the whole armor of God, that you may be able to stand against the schemes of the devil. For we do not wrestle against flesh and blood, but against the rulers, against the authorities, against the cosmic powers over this present darkness, against the spiritual forces of evil in the heavenly places. Therefore take up the whole armor of God, that you may be able to withstand in the evil day, and having done all, to stand firm. (Eph. 6:11–13)

Withstand means "to be against something or someone; to oppose or resist something with great resolve." The enemy that we *withstand* is not a physical enemy. "We do not wrestle with flesh and blood," as Paul says (Eph. 6:12). We are called to *withstand* rulers, authorities, cosmic powers over this present darkness, and spiritual forces of evil in the heavenly places. The only way we stand firm and *withstand* the enemy is by putting on the whole armor of God.

We are called to fight with all our might against sin and Satan. Our only hope for fighting such a battle is by wearing the full armor of God. A.W. Pink writes, "It is called the 'armor of God' because he both provides it and bestows it, for we have none of our own; and yet, while this armor is of God's providing and bestowing, we have to put in on! This means we must put into action the graces God has given us in Christ."[1] Spiritual soldiers have much to gain by wearing the whole armor of God. First, *every soldier who wears the armor of God is standing, which as we have seen, is the proper posture for the spiritual battle.*

Second, *every soldier who wears the armor of God is obeying God.* If you are opposing God in any way, you are not wearing the armor. If you are resisting God in any way, you are not wearing the armor. And if you are defying God in any way, you are not wearing the armor.

Third, *every soldier who wears the armor of God is adequately protected.* We will learn that the armor protects us from anything and everything that the enemy sends our way.

Fourth, *every soldier who wears the armor of God will be properly prepared for warfare.* This is vitally important as the enemy will use a host of tactics on the field of battle:

- He attempts to distort the character of God (Gen. 3).
- He attempts to deceive us (2 Cor. 11:14).
- He attempts to disorient us by confusing us about doctrine (Eph. 4:14).

- He attempts to divide us.
- He attempts to delude us by convincing us to wallow in our guilt (Rom. 5:1).
- He attempts to create doubt in us and take away our confidence in the promises of God.
- He attempts to dupe us with worldly pleasures (1 John 2:15-17).
- He attempts to distort the truth.

As we open the war chest, we will soon discover the individual pieces of armor and the benefit they bring us in the Christian life. But before we pry open that war chest, notice three things by way of introduction:

First, *there is a specific order*. That is, one piece of armor comes before another by way of design. Ray Stedman observes, "You cannot alter the order in any way. For example, the reason many Christians fail to exercise the sword of the Spirit is that they have never first girded up their loins with the truth. You cannot do this in reverse order. Scripture is very exact on this."[2]

Second, *the armor is Christ*. "The armor is nothing more than a symbolic description of the Lord himself. The armor is Christ and what he is prepared to be and to do in each one of us ... It is not merely Christ available to us, but Christ actually appropriated."[3]

Third, *our strength is found in Christ*. "God is our strength," writes John MacArthur, "but His strength is appropriated only through obedience; His mighty armor must be put on and taken up."[4] We begin, therefore, with the belt of truth.

A CLEAR DESCRIPTION

The belt of truth is the necessary starting place in our preparation for the battlefield. Apart from truth we have no basis with which to live the Christian life. Apart from truth we wander aimlessly and are vulnerable to attack of the enemy.

The belt of truth supplies us with the essential information that is necessary to live the Christian life.[5] It tells us who God is. He is the Creator (Gen. 1:1; Ps. 90:2; Prov. 8:22-23, 27-30). Albert M. Wolters adds, "The almighty Creator lays claim to it all; the universal Sovereign lays down his laws for it all; the absolute King requires his will to be discerned in it all."[6]

The belt of truth tells us who we are. We are creatures made in the image of God who fell from God (Gen. 1:27; Rom. 3:23; 5:12; Isa. 43:7). Wolters continues:

> Sin, an alien invasion of creation, is completely foreign to God's purposes for his creatures. It was not meant to be; it simply does not belong. Any theory that somehow sanctions the existence of evil in God's good creation fails to do justice to sin's fundamentally outrageous and blasphemous character, and in some subtle or sophisticated sense lays the blame for sin on the Creator rather than on ourselves in Adam.[7]

The belt of truth tells us what God has done. Christ is the Redeemer. "For even the Son of Man came not to be served but to serve, and to give his life as a ransom for many" (Mark 10:45; c.f. Rom. 3:24-25; Col. 1:19-20).

Apart from the belt of truth, we are lost in the world, without God, and without hope. Apart from the belt of truth, we don't know who God is, we don't know who we are, and we don't know what God has done for us in Christ.

A COLOSSAL CHALLENGE

From the beginning, God has always spoken authoritatively. "God's authority," writes John Frame, "is his right to command, his right to tell us what we ought to do. When he issues commands, he is supremely right in doing so. Thus, his word creates for us an obligation to obey."[8] To question the authority of an omnipotent God is an asinine enterprise. Yet, we see a pattern running throughout redemptive history where people constantly challenge God's right to rule and his sovereign authority. This pattern continues to this day with a vengeance.

The serpent was the first to question God's authority and the truth claims that the Creator utters. The serpent asks Eve, "Did God actually say, 'You shall not eat of any tree in the Garden'" (Gen. 3:1). Next, the serpent makes a bold assertion in Eve's presence: "You shall not surely die. For God knows that when you eat of it your eyes will be opened, and you will be like God, knowing good and evil" (Gen. 3:5). The serpent's lie was a brazen challenge to God's authority – and Eve knew it.

Challenging God's authority and his claim to the truth has been taking place since the dawn of creation. The history of western philosophy is no exception. In the ancient (pre-modern) period, God's authority was consistently challenged. "Thinkers began to develop their thinking outside of, and independent from, a biblical framework. The medieval synthesis of Christian and Greek thought had started to unravel."[9]

In the modern period, reason replaced revelation, autonomy replaced authority, deism replaced theism, and man replaced God. "The goal of the 'Enlightenment project' was to free humanity from superstition and found a philosophy and civilization on rational inquiry, empirical evidence and scientific discovery."[10]

In the postmodern period, a single worldview and overarching meta-narrative is rejected. John MacArthur sums up the mindset that dominates the postmodern ethos:

> Postmodernism in general is marked by a tendency to dismiss the possibility of any sure and settled knowledge of the truth. Postmodernism suggests that if objective truth exists, it cannot be known objectively or with any degree of certainty ... Strong convictions about any point of truth are judged supremely as arrogant and hopelessly naïve. Everyone is entitled to his own truth.[11]

Postmodern thinkers, therefore, discard the notion of absolute truth and replace it with a radical allegiance to relativism. Francis Schaeffer addressed these concerns over fifty years ago as he bore witness to the rise of postmodernity. He summarizes this colossal challenge in his popular book, *The God Who is There*:

> The present chasm between the generations has been brought about almost entirely by a change in the concept of truth ... The tragedy of our situation today is that men and women are being fundamentally affected by the new way of looking at truth, and yet they have never analyzed the drift which has taken place ... So this change in the concept of the way we come to knowledge and truth is the most crucial problem, as I understand it, facing Christianity today.[12]

The issue that Schaeffer identified in the 1960's continues to wreak havoc in the church today. I speak frequently to college students who question the viability of "truth claims" at best or abandon the possibility of absolute truth claims entirely. Such a pursuit is not logically consistent and fails the practical test of living in the real world.

A CRITICAL DIRECTION

Scripture charges us with two critical directives. First, *we must gird our loins with truth*. *Fastened* (ESV) and *girded* (NASB) mean "to fasten with a belt to secure clothing and prepare for war." A Roman solider would wear a tunic which draped over his body. Since much of the warfare in those days was hand-to-hand combat, a loose tunic posed a major problem. So before the battle began, the tunic was cinched up and tucked into a leather belt that girded his loins.[13]

Girding our loins, then, represents one who is spiritually prepared:

> Therefore gird up the loins of your mind, be sober, and rest your hope fully upon the grace that is to be brought to you at the revelation of Jesus Christ. (1 Peter 1:13, NKJV)

Truth (*àleitheia*) is a "message that conforms to reality." We are called to fasten the belt of truth; to gird our loins with the belt of truth. There is no question that *àleitheia* points to content, as we have already seen. But it also indicates a need to live truthfully. When we come to the sword of the Spirit (Eph. 6:17), we will delve deeply into truth as it relates to content. But truth in this context refers primarily to our commitment to live truthfully. Notice how the English Standard Version translates our passage.

> Therefore, preparing your minds for action, and being sober-minded, set your hope fully on the grace that will be brought to you at the revelation of Jesus Christ." (1 Peter 1:13)

Ask yourself a few critical questions:

1. Am I spiritually prepared?

2. Am I a person committed to the truth?

3. Do I believe the truth?

4. Do I have strong convictions concerning the truth?

5. Am I willing to lay down my life for the cause of truth?

The mind of a battle-ready soldier is always prepared for action.

Second, *we must guard our minds with truth*. Gresham Machen understood this principle well and was one of the most stalwart defenders of the faith in the twentieth century. Machen argued, "False ideas are the greatest obstacles to the reception of the gospel."[14] As battle-ready soldiers, we must therefore, steer clear from false teaching (1 Tim. 6:20-21). We must avoid being intimidated by false teachers (Matt. 7:15; 2 Tim. 4:14-15). And we must avoid being carried away by propagators of heresy (2 Pet. 3:17; Acts 20:29-30).

Have you girded your loins with the truth? Are you guarding your mind with the truth? How do you know if the belt of truth is securely fastened?

- The truth of God's Word guides your steps.

- The truth of God's Word dictates your actions.
- The truth of God's Word controls your affections.
- The truth of God's Word informs your conscience.
- The truth of God's Word governs your lips.
- The truth of God's Word motivates your heart.
- The truth of God's Word is the highest authority in your life. You refuse to compromise the truth.

Fastening the *belt of truth* places you in a posture of spiritual readiness. When you fasten the *belt of truth*, you are committing yourself to ordering your life according to the Word of God. You have no other allegiances. God's Word is your highest authority.

Go into the battlefield prepared! When you wear the *belt of truth*, you are ready for action. When you wear the *belt of truth*, your disposition is focused on God. When you wear the *belt of truth*, your attitude is fixated on Christ and his completed work on the cross. When you wear the *belt of truth*, your desires are Godward. When you wear the *belt of truth*, your commitments, convictions, and your conduct are properly aligned. You practice what you preach. You live truthfully!

Are you prepared for battle? The battle is raging all around us. It will continue to rage until Christ returns and makes all things new. In the meantime, we wait patiently and live for God's glory. Have you girded your loins with truth? If you are not yet a follower of Christ, your first move is to confess that *he is the truth!* Once you acknowledge that Jesus is the truth, confess your sin to him and receive the saving benefits of his life, death, burial, and resurrection. Then and only then will you have right-standing with God and stand forgiven before him.

Oh, follower of Christ – God has given you the *belt of truth*. I urge you to gird your loins with truth. I urge you to guard your mind with truth. I plead with you to go into the battlefield, prepared. May you live truthfully, without hypocrisy and without pretense. And may you bear witness to God who is the very essence of truth!

---

1. A.W. Pink, Practical Christianity, 124.
2. Ray Stedman, Spiritual Warfare (Portland: Multnomah Press, 1975), 74.
3. Ibid., 72.
4. John F. MacArthur, Ephesians (Chicago: Moody Press, 1986), 343.
5. Note the basic components of the Christian worldview: creation, fall, and redemption. It is easy to take these components for granted. Imagine where we would be without a knowledge of the truth!
6. Albert M. Wolters, Creation Regained: Biblical Basis for a Reformational Worldview (Grand Rapids: Eerdmans, 1985), 15.
7. Ibid., 49.
8. John M. Frame, The Doctrine of God (Phillipsburg: P&R, 2002), 80.
9. Douglas Groothuis, Truth Decay (Downers Grove: IVP, 2000), 34.
10. Alasdair MacIntyre, After Virtue: A Study in Moral Theory, 2nd ed. (Notre Dame: University of Notre Dame Press, 1984), Cited in Ibid, 35.
11. John F. MacArthur, The Truth War (Nashville: Thomas Nelson, 2007), 10-11.
12. Francis A. Schaeffer, The God Who is There (Downers Grove: IVP, 1968), 5-6.
13. See MacArthur, Ephesians, 348-349.
14. J. Gresham Machen: A Biographical Memoir, 389.

6

The Breastplate of Righteousness

Righteousness and holiness are God's protection to defend the believer's conscience from all wounds inflicted by sin.

WILLIAM GURNALL

Every disciple of Jesus Christ is in an intense struggle. We have been looking at this struggle and have seen that it may involve discouragement. It may involve depression. It may involve doubt. The moment we commit to serving Christ, we enter a battlefield that is both spiritual and intense. It is a battle that never lets up. God's Word instructs us:

> Finally, be strong in the Lord and in the strength of his might. Put on the whole armor of God, that you may be able to stand against the schemes of the devil. For we do not wrestle against flesh and blood, but against the rulers, against the authorities, against the cosmic powers over this present darkness, against the spiritual forces of evil in the heavenly places. Therefore take up the whole armor of God, that you may be able to withstand in the evil day, and having done all, to stand firm. (Eph. 6:10–13)

Battle-ready saints always stand firm. Battle-ready saints never surrender. In Ephesians 6:14, we are instructed to "fasten on the belt of truth." We are also instructed to "put on the breastplate of righteousness." That is the focus of this chapter.

A RIGHTEOUSNESS THAT COULD ONLY COME FROM GOD

In ancient days, a Roman soldier would strap on his breastplate before marching onto the battlefield. The breastplate was an armor plate with straps of leather or linen that not only protected the chest; it covered the body from the neck to the thighs. It had two parts – one to protect the front and one to protect the back. The breastplate, then, was an essential piece of armor for the Roman soldier.

Paul has in mind the image of a Roman soldier in Ephesians 6. But when he refers to the breastplate, he's not talking about any ol' breastplate. He's talking about the breastplate of righteousness. Righteousness (*dikaiosúnei*) is "a status of legal rectitude that satisfies the moral requirements of God's character." It conforms to the claims of a higher authority.

The fundamental idea of righteousness is that of strict adherence to the law. It presupposes that there is a law to which we must conform. The Hebrew terms for "righteous" and "righteousness" are *tsaddik*, tsedhek, and tsedhakah. The corresponding Greek terms, *dikaios* and *dikaiosune*, all contains the idea of conformity to a standard.

God is righteous

The righteousness of God is a theme that literally dominates the Scriptures. Beginning in the Old Testament, we learn that God is all-together righteous:

> O LORD, the God of Israel, you are just, for we are left a remnant that has escaped, as it is today.

> Behold, we are before you in our guilt, for none can stand before you because of this. (Ezra 9:15)
>
> Righteous are you, O LORD, and right are your rules. (Ps. 119:137)
>
> The LORD is righteous in all his ways and kind in all his works. (Ps. 145:17)
>
> Therefore the LORD has kept ready the calamity and has brought it upon us, for the LORD our God is righteous in all the works that he has done, and we have not obeyed his voice. (Dan.9:14)

The New Testament picks up where the Old Testament left off and reveals that God is a righteous judge and calls his people to follow him in his stead:

> Henceforth there is laid up for me the crown of righteousness, which the Lord, the righteous judge, will award to me on that day, and not only to me but also to all who have loved his appearing. (2 Tim. 4:8)
>
> If you know that he is righteous, you may be sure that everyone who practices righteousness has been born of him. (1 John 2:29)
>
> Little children, let no one deceive you. Whoever practices righteousness is righteous, as he is righteous. (1 John 3:7)
>
> And I heard the angel in charge of the waters say, 'Just are you, O Holy One, who is and who was, for you brought these judgments.' (Rev. 16:5)

God demands us to be righteous

> Therefore the wicked will not stand in the judgment, nor sinners in the congregation of the righteous; for the LORD knows the way of the righteous, but the way of the wicked will perish. (Ps. 1:5–6)

We can never be righteous on our own merits

> We have all become like one who is unclean, and all our righteous deeds are like a polluted garment. We all fade like a leaf, and our iniquities, like the wind, take us away. (Isa. 64:6)

We need the righteousness of Another

It is only by faith in the Lord Jesus Christ and his completed work on the cross that we can be forgiven of all our sin and be credited with his righteousness. This righteousness can only come from God through Christ.

DISTINGUISHING RIGHTEOUSNESS

Imputed Righteousness

The only way that we can receive the righteousness of God, according to Scripture, is by grace alone through faith alone. Nothing more, nothing less. Justification is "that act by which unjust sinners are made right in the sight of a just and holy God ... We are declared, counted, or reckoned to be righteous when God imputes the righteousness of Christ to our account."[1]

> Now to the one who works, his wages are not counted as a gift but as his due. And to the one who does not work but believes in him who justifies the ungodly, his faith is counted as righteousness ... (Rom. 4:4–5)
>
> For our sake he made him to be sin who knew no sin, so that in him we might become the righteousness of God. (2 Cor. 5:21)

Paul is not referring to imputed righteousness when he instructs us to put on the breastplate of righteousness. Here's the reason: *God has already imputed the righteousness of Christ to our account!* And so, Paul is not referring to imputed righteousness in Ephesians 6:14; he's referring to imparted righteousness. "Imputed righteousness is what Christ works for the believer, the justification which lets him stand righteous before God ... imparted righteousness is what Christ works in the believer."[2]

Imparted Righteousness

John MacArthur helps us understand this vital lesson: "God Himself puts on our imputed righteousness, but we must put on our practical righteousness."[3] This means that we have a significant responsibility as followers of Christ:

> Therefore, my beloved, as you have always obeyed, so now, not only as in my presence but much more in my absence, work out your own salvation with fear and trembling, for it is God who works in you, both to will and to work for his good pleasure. (Phil. 2:12–13)
>
> I have been crucified with Christ. It is no longer I who live, but Christ who lives in me. And the life I now live in the flesh I live by faith in the Son

> of God, who loved me and gave himself for me. (Gal. 2:20)
>
> As obedient children, do not be conformed to the passions of your former ignorance, but as he who called you is holy, you also be holy in all your conduct. (1 Pet.1:14–15)
>
> Beloved, I urge you as sojourners and exiles to abstain from the passions of the flesh, which wage war against your soul. (1 Pet. 2:11)

Imputed righteousness (positional righteousness), then, is what Christ works for us, the justification which enables us to stand righteous before God. *Imparted righteousness* (practical righteousness) is what Christ works in us.

God commands us to put on the breastplate of righteousness. There are no "couch potatoes" on the battlefield. John MacArthur reminds us, "Imputed righteousness makes practical righteousness possible, but only obedience to the Lord makes practical righteousness a reality."[4]

We must, therefore, put on the breastplate of righteousness that militates against every ounce of self-effort (Rom. 4:5; Isa. 64:6; Eph. 2:9). We must put on the breastplate of righteousness that annihilates every form of anti-gospel. Praise God for the righteousness of Christ that is sufficient to protect us in the spiritual battle.

1. R.C. Sproul, Essential Truths of the Christian Faith (Wheaton: Tyndale House Publishers, 1988), 189.
2. William Gurnall, The Christian in Complete Armour, 144-145.
3. John F. MacArthur, Ephesians (Chicago: Moody Press, 1986), 353.
4. Ibid., 352.

7

The Shoes of the Gospel of Peace

May the LORD give strength to his people! May the LORD bless his people with peace!

PSALM 29:11

A solitary sculpture sits in the beautiful city of Geneva, Switzerland. This captivating piece of art portrays a person slumped over, obviously racked with grief. A massive hole is carved out in the center of the sculpture, representing the void that people have when they experience loss or pain. The name of the sculpture is *Melancholy*. Albert György created this stunning sculpture as a way of coping with profound isolation and sadness after the death of his wife.

The response to György's creative work was nothing short of remarkable. Soon after his masterpiece was unveiled, encouraging responses began to pour in. Many were posted online. His transparency helped others cope with the sadness, grief, and loss that they too had recently experienced. György's artistic talent struck an unexpected nerve.

György's work not only resonated with hurting people; it was a vivid reminder of the intense need people have for peace. Tragically, peace eludes most people. Instead of traveling on a path of peace like God intends, people pursue anything but

God's best. This subversion of God's perfect plan might seem logical in the short run to the sinful creature. Scripture says, "There is a way that seems right to a man, but its end is the way to death" (Prov. 14:12). Cornelius Plantinga Jr. comments on God's attitude toward this creaturely rebellion: "God hates sin not just because it violates his law but, more substantively, because it violates shalom, because it breaks the peace, because it interferes with the way things are supposed to be ... In short, sin is culpable shalom-breaking."[1]

God intends that his creatures live in peace. Every person who places faith in Jesus Christ actually experiences peace with God. The Bible not only prescribes peace with God; it points the way for every creature to find this peace. It is what one might a call a spiritual feast for the soul.

A SPIRITUAL FEAST FOR THE SOUL

The apostle Paul begins Romans 5 with these monumental words:

> Therefore, since we have been justified by faith, we have peace with God through our Lord Jesus Christ. (Rom. 5:1)

It is justification that paves the path to peace for every believing person. This peace is crucial to understand and embrace in our fight against sin. Notice seven crucial realities about the miracle of justification.

The miracle of justification

First, *it is a declaration*. The word translated as *justified* in Romans 5:1 means "to set right; to vindicate; to declare righteous." When we place our faith and trust in Christ, God declares us righteous. To be clear: Justification does not *make* us righteous. It does not begin a process where we become righteous at some point. Rather, justification is a declaration of our new status before God. Martyn Lloyd-Jones writes, "Justification makes no actual change in us; it is a declaration by God concerning us."[2] Justification, then, is a pronouncement about our new standing before a holy God.

Second, *it is a legal action*. It is forensic. Justification is a term that comes from the court of law. R.C. Sproul provides a helpful definition: "Justification may be defined as that act by which unjust sinners are made right in the sight of a just and holy God."[3] James White adds, "To be justified means to be declared right with God by virtue of the remission of sins accomplished by Jesus; Christ's righteousness is imputed to the believer, and the believer's sins are imputed to Christ, who bears them in his body on the tree."[4]

All those who place their faith in Christ, then, are declared righteous. If you have trusted Christ, you are no longer God's enemy. You are his friend. Instead of falling under the holy wrath of God, you are acquitted. When you are justified, you are cleansed from all your sins - past, present, and future! This legal action is an ironclad declaration by God.

Third, *it is a divine action*. Justification is the work of almighty God. He planned it, and he initiates it. Theologians refer to this as the divine initiative.

> But I with the voice of thanksgiving will sacrifice to you; what I have vowed I will pay. Salvation belongs to the LORD! (Jonah 2:9)
>
> You did not choose me, but I chose you and appointed you that you should go and bear fruit and that your fruit should abide, so that whatever you ask the Father in my name, he may give it to you. (John 15:16).

God took the first step in our salvation. He gets the credit. He gets the glory.

Fourth, *it is an accomplished fact.* The Greek word translated as *justified* in Romans 5:1 is an aorist tense verb. It refers to an action that happened at a point in time. That is why we refer to justification as an accomplished reality, not a work in progress. Justification is not a process. It is a sovereign act of God that occurs in real time and real space.

So there are only two kinds of people — justified people and unjustified people. Some people are right with God; some people are at war with God. Some people stand innocent before the bar of God's justice; other people stand condemned before a holy God. The critical questions for you to consider are these:

- Are you right with God?
- Have you been justified?

Fifth, *it is a secure fact.* Justification is a once-for-all action on the part of God. "One who is justified cannot become 'unjustified,' for all the believer's sins have been forgiven on the basis of the work of Christ."[5] C.H. Spurgeon says:

> No true child of God perishes – hold that fast; but this is the badge of a true child of God, - that a man endures to the end, and if a man does not hold on, but slinks back to his old master, and once again fits on the old collar, and wears again the Satanic yoke, there is sure proof that he has never come out of the spiritual Egypt through Jesus Christ, his leader, and hath never obtained that eternal life which cannot die, because it is born of God.[6]

There are many uncertainties in this life. Praise God that our justification is a secure fact. Our salvation is secure for all eternity.

Sixth, *it is a gift.* We are justified by God's grace as a gift. Ephesians 2:4-5 says, "But God, being rich in mercy, because of the great love with which he loved us, even when we were dead in our trespasses, made us alive together with Christ — by grace you have been saved." By definition, a gift can never be earned or purchased. Justification is a gracious gift from a sovereign and merciful God.

Seventh, *it is received by faith alone.* "Therefore, since we have been justified by faith, we have peace with God through our Lord Jesus Christ" (Rom. 5:1). To have faith is to trust Christ. John MacArthur writes, "The call of Calvary must be recognized for what it is; a call to discipleship under the lordship of Jesus Christ. To respond to that call is to become a believer. Anything less is simply unbelief."[7] Therefore, trusting Christ means believing in Christ. When we believe in Christ, we surrender to him. We bank all our hope on Christ. We submit to his sovereign authority. We obey him. We demonstrate our allegiance to him. And we fight sin all the way to the Celestial City.

Oh, reader, do you believe? Have you turned from your sin and turned to Jesus for salvation? Have you received the miracle of justification? Have you abandoned every attempt at so-called "righteousness" and trusted God to declare you righteous? Call upon the name of the Lord and you will be saved (Acts 16:31).

I encourage Christian readers who struggle with doubt and wrestle with assurance about justification to bank on the facts. Believe the promises of God. Trust the Word of God. If you are a Christian, I urge you to delight in the first course of the spiritual feast for the soul. This is the miracle of justification.

The merriment of justification

The second course in this spiritual feast is the merriment of justification. The word *merriment* implies cheerfulness or joy. We will discover that justification is the root cause of this joy. Romans 5:1 says, "We have peace with God." In the Old Testament, *peace* is what people longed for. *Peace* is blessing or favor that comes directly from the hand of God. The Hebrew word, *shalom* means "welfare, prosperity, or wholeness." In Old Testament times, peace was paramount for Jewish people. Theologically, *peace* expresses a relationship of love and loyalty between the Creator and the creature.

> The LORD bless you and keep you; the LORD make his face to shine upon you and be gracious to you; the LORD lift up his countenance upon you and give you peace. (Numb. 6:24–26)

In the New Testament, peace means harmonious relations and freedom from disputes; freedom from worry. "This peace," writes Martin Luther, "consists in an appeased conscience and in confidence in God, just as conversely the lack of peace means spiritual anxiety, a disturbed conscience and mistrust over against God."[8] Luther's comments about those who are devoid of peace accurately describe the condition of people in our culture who are plagued with anxiety and clamor for relief.

The most contentious relationship in the cosmos is between sinners and a holy God. Unconverted sinners are enemies of God and at war with him (Rom. 5:10). They willfully violate his law and walk on a sinful path. Each sinner, then, is under the wrath of God (Col. 3:5-8). Yet, notice the mighty hope found in Romans 5:1.

> Therefore, since we have been justified by faith, we have peace with God through our Lord Jesus Christ.

Three biblical realities directly apply to every person who has placed faith in the Lord Jesus Christ. First, *we have peace with God*. "We shall never know 'the peace of God' until we have 'peace with God.'"[9] The war between sinners and God must come to a halt. That is only possible when sinners are justified. When we place our faith in Christ, we have peace with God.

Second, *we have peace with God now.*[10] We are not waiting to experience peace with God now. The enmity is over! We are reconciled to God. "The peace that a believer has in the knowledge that he is secure forever in Christ not only strengthens his faith but strengthens his service."[11] Praise God for the peace that every follower of Christ enjoys this very moment.

Third, *this peace is supernatural*. Because we have peace with God (objective), we have the peace of God (subjective). The apostle Paul writes, "And the peace of God, which surpasses all understanding, will guard your hearts and minds in Christ Jesus" (Phil. 4:7, CSB). This peace calms the anxious soul. This peace stills the turbulent mind. This peace sets our feet on a path of Godward tranquility. This peace has no fear of judgment. This peace has no fear of death. Hebrews 2:14 says, "Since therefore the children share in flesh and blood, he himself likewise partook of the same things, that through death he might destroy the one who has the power of death, that is, the devil." The one who is justified by faith alone can joyfully sing with Toplady:

> The terrors of the law and of God, with me can have nothing to do; My Savior's obedience and blood hide all my transgressions from view.[12]

Praise God for his mercy and grace. Praise the Lord for the forgiveness he freely extends to every person who places trust in Christ. And praise the Triune God for freely granting peace to fallen sinners. This is the merriment of justification!

The means of justification

Romans 5:1 tells us that justification is "through the Lord Jesus Christ." Romans 3:23-24 says, "For all have sinned and fall short of the glory of God, and are justified by his grace as a gift, through the redemption that is in Christ Jesus." *The New City Catechism* provides an inside look at the beauty of justification:

> Q 20: Who is the redeemer?
>
> A: The only Redeemer is the Lord Jesus Christ, the eternal son of God, in whom God became man and bore the penalty of sin himself.[13]
>
> Q 25: Does Christ's death mean all our sins can be forgiven?
>
> A: Yes, because Christ's death on the cross fully paid the penalty for our sin, God graciously imputes Christ's righteousness to us as if it were our own and will remember our sin no more.[14]

We do not receive right standing with God by good works. We do not receive right standing with God by being religious or attending church services. We receive right standing with God by grace alone, through faith alone, in Christ alone! This is the good news. It is not only good news; it is the greatest news! So stop trying to impress God. Put your candles away. Get rid of your religious paraphernalia. Trust in Christ alone and his completed work on the cross.

We have focused our attention in this chapter on the miracle of justification, the merriment of justification, and the means of justification. Truly, this is a spiritual feast for the soul. Now that we have a better understanding of the peace that we enjoy as followers of Christ, we are in a position of understanding the next piece of armor in our fight against sin.

A SPIRITUAL SHOE FOR WARFARE

So far, we have seen that God calls us to put on the belt of truth. He instructs us to put on the breastplate of righteousness. The next piece of armor is also defensive in nature, namely - the shoes of the gospel of peace. As we saw above, the only way to receive this peace is by being justified by faith alone.

No one enters the battlefield without shoes. To enter the field of battle in a shoeless condition would imply a lack of readiness and a foolish disposition. Shoes imply a state of readiness. *Having put on* (*úpodéō*) means "to bind sandals." The aorist tense verb indicates a point in time action that takes place in our lives. If my family decides to go downtown for dinner and we make plans to leave at 5:30 p.m. and one of my kids notice that I have not yet put my shoes on, it indicates one thing: I'm not ready! Paul instructs believers, "For shoes, put on the peace that comes from the Good News so that you will be fully prepared" (Eph. 6:15, NLT).

The English Standard Version translates verse 15 as follows: "and, as shoes for your feet, having put on the readiness given by the gospel of peace. *Readiness* (*étoimasía*) means "the state of being ready or prepared for action."

Wearing shoes on the battlefield implies a proper mindset, one of readiness. Wearing the shoes points to a saint who is right with God. Before we came to faith in Christ, we were enemies of God (Rom. 5:10) and strangers to the promises of God (Eph. 2:12). Indeed, we were under the wrath of God (Rom. 1:18-19; 2:5). Everyone who places their faith in Christ has peace with God.

In our fight against sin, it is essential that we remember our new status with God. We enjoy *positional* peace with God and we enjoy *practical* peace with God. This astounding reality helps us in our battle against sin. William Gurnall reminds us, "Christian, there is only one way to stop the invasion of sin. To steel your heart against all compromise with evil you must carry the Savior's blood into the battle with your hand of faith."[15] We are the blood-bought children of God who have peace with God. Praise God that we not only stand secure in Christ; we are prepared for spiritual battle.

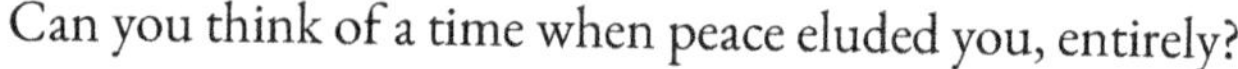

Can you think of a time when peace eluded you, entirely?

- Your mind is tormented by a conflicted conscience.
- Your soul is battered by temptation.
- Your heart is wounded because someone close to you died.
- You live in a constant state of tension.

Now is the time to apply the benefits of the gospel to your life on a daily basis. Now is the time for you to put on the shoes of the gospel of peace.

György's artistic work is a great encouragement for struggling souls. But a sculpture can only bring temporary rest. I recently met a young man who admitted that he struggled with thanatophobia. While I had never heard the term, I was familiar with the words "thanatos" (death) and "phobia" (fear). I responded, "I understand. The fear of death is very real for many people." Every person needs the peace of God, which is found only through faith in the Lord Jesus Christ.

Every disciple of Jesus Christ is engaged in an intense struggle. But God has given us the armor, which protects us in every way. The Bible says, "Therefore, since we have been justified by faith, we have peace with God through our Lord Jesus Christ" (Rom. 5:1). You need to enter the battlefield properly equipped. You need to fasten the belt of truth. You need to put on the breastplate of righteousness. And you need to wear the shoes of the gospel of peace. All of these things place you in a posture of *spiritual readiness!*

> Finally, be strong in the Lord and in the strength of his might. Put on the whole armor of God, that you may be able to stand against the schemes of the devil. For we do not wrestle against flesh and blood, but against the rulers, against the authorities, against the cosmic powers over this present darkness, against the spiritual forces of evil in the heavenly places. Therefore take up the whole armor of God, that you may be able to withstand in the evil day, and having done all, to stand firm. (Eph. 6:10–13)

---

1. Cornelius Plantinga Jr., Not the Way It's Supposed to Be: A Breviary of Sin (Grand Rapids: Eerdmans Publishing Company, 1995), 14.
2. Martyn Lloyd-Jones, Romans: Exposition of Chapter 3:20-4:25, Atonement and Justification (Edinburgh: Banner of Truth, 1970), 55.
3. R.C. Sproul, Essential Truths of the Christian Faith (Wheaton: Tyndale, 1998), 189.
4. James White, The God Who Justifies: The Doctrine of Justification (Minneapolis: Bethany House, 2001), 73.
5. Ibid., 68.

6. C.H. Spurgeon, Spurgeon's Sermons: Volume 8 - Enduring to the End (Grand Rapids: Baker Book House, 1883), 161-162.
7. John MacArthur, The Gospel According to Jesus (Grand Rapids: Zondervan, 1998), 46.
8. Martin Luther, Commentary on Romans (Grand Rapids: Kregel Publications, 1954), 89.
9. Martyn Lloyd-Jones, Romans: Exposition of Chapter 5, Assurance (Edinburgh: Banner of Truth, 1971), 13.
10. Peace with God is objective. The peace of God is subjective and helps believers overcome anxiety and despair (Phil. 4:7).
11. John MacArthur, Romans 1-8 (Chicago: Moody Press, 1991), 275.
12. Augustus M. Toplady, A Debtor to Mercy Alone.
13. The New City Catechism (Wheaton: Crossway Books, 2017), 44-45.
14. Ibid., 66-67.
15. Gurnall, The Christian in Complete Armour, 2:298.

8

The Shield of Faith

Now faith is the assurance of things hoped for, the conviction of things not seen.

HEBREWS 11:1

For some time now, the United States has been preoccupied with the possibility of a nuclear attack from North Korea. For years, the rogue nation has been "flexing their muscles" and have even suggested that the technology is in place that could successfully launch a nuclear warhead on the American mainland.

In 2017 I read an article in the *Washington Post* entitled, "If North Korea Fires a Nuclear Missile at the U.S., How Could it Be Stopped?"[1] The lead sentence in the article began: "North Korea can make a nuclear bomb and has an intercontinental ballistic missile capable of reaching the U.S. mainland. If it launches such a missile, the United States has a $40 billion system designed to destroy the bomb in space." It is the next line, however, that caught my attention: "*What is unknown is whether it will succeed.*" The article proceeded to show how this system works:

- North Korea launches an intercontinental ballistic missile (ICBM).

- Satellites and radar detect and track it.
- The missile releases the warhead - and decoys.
- Interceptors launched, which releases a "kill vehicle."
- The kill vehicle picks out the warhead and slams into the warhead and destroys it.[2]

The *Washington Post* piece concludes with these chilling words:

> If North Korea sent six ICBM warheads at the United Sates and we got five of them, you'd say, 'Hey, five out of six, not bad,' said Bruce W. MacDonald, former assistant director for national security at the White House Office of Science and Technology Policy. 'But if you ended up losing Seattle ... you'd still feel pretty bad even though it was over 80 percent effective.'[3]

Thankfully, we have not had to endure such an attack. Yet, the Bible tells us that Satan consistently launches his flaming darts at followers of Christ. But the Bible also tells us about our defense against these attacks. The apostle Paul instructs us to take up the shield of faith: "In all circumstances *take up* the *shield of faith*, with which you can extinguish all the flaming darts of the evil one ..." (Eph. 6:16). Notice six descriptive words that help us understand the shield of faith:

COVERING

The word translated as *shield* (*thureós*) means "an oblong shield." It is used in the Old Testament as a handheld barrier of self-defense:

> You mountains of Gilboa, let there be no dew or rain upon you, nor fields of offerings! For there the shield of the mighty was defiled, the shield of Saul, not anointed with oil. (2 Sam. 1:21)

> The shaft of his spear was like a weaver's beam, and his spear's head weighed six hundred shekels of iron. And his shield-bearer went before him. (1 Sam. 17:7)

> The shield of his mighty men is red; his soldiers are clothed in scarlet. The chariots come with flashing metal on the day he musters them; the cypress spears are brandished. (Nah. 2:3)

We will see that this shield has a specific purpose, namely, to "extinguish all the flaming darts of the evil one" (Eph. 6:16).

COMITTMENT

Paul tells the Ephesians to *take up* (*ànalambànō*) the shield of faith. The term comes from a Greek word that means "to take and lift upward; to acquire; to seize; to grasp." But it is the tense of the verb that is especially significant. *Take up* appears in the aorist tense, which stresses a point-in-time decision to acquire or to literally *take up* the shield of faith.

Our commitment, then, to taking up the shield of faith requires strong resolution. It requires boldness. It requires obedience. Our commitment to taking up the shield of faith requires courage. Like the other pieces of armor that we've already seen, there is no negotiating here. We are called to take up the shield of faith. The very act requires decisive commitment on our part.

What is preventing you from taking up the shield of faith? Can you pinpoint what is preventing you from being fully committed in this regard? What steps of obedience can you take right now to demonstrate your passion to engage in holy war for the glory of God?

COMPREHENSIVE

Paul instructs the Ephesians and all subsequent believers to take up the shield of faith in all (*pas*) circumstances. That is, no matter what we face, we are called to take up the shield of faith:

> In every situation take up the shield of faith with which you can extinguish all the flaming arrows of the evil one. (Eph. 6:16, CSB)

We take up the shield of faith at school. We take up the shield of faith at home and at work. We take up the shield of faith on vacation. We take up the shield of faith when we are tempted. We take up the shield of faith when we are discouraged or plagued with anxiety. We take up the shield of faith in moments of adversity. *In all circumstances, we take up the shield of faith!*

CRITICAL

Without the shield of faith, we are open game on the battlefield. When a solider neglects his shield on the field of battle, he is open to the enemies' attack. Without the shield of faith, we are not only exposed to our enemy; we actually invite the attack of the enemy.

Scripture says that the devil hurls "flaming darts" (ESV) at the people of God. The New American Standard Bible and the Christian Standard Bible translate the Greek word *bélos* as "flaming arrows." In other words, these arrows or missiles are sent in our direction. They are flaming. They are hot. These warheads sent directly from behind the enemy lines are intense!

3 examples of *bélos*

The enemy of our souls launches an array of flaming arrows in our direction. First, *notice the missile of deception*. The devil wants to trick us. He wants to confuse us. He wants us to fall prey to the seeds of confusion he sows. He wants us to minimize doctrine. He wants us to set theology aside. He wants us to grow fascinated with the things of this world. He will do anything to get us to think about what we might gain by being worldly. In short, he will do anything to prevent us from pursuing a godly life.

The apostle Paul had a friend named Demas who was deceived by the devil (2 Tim. 4:10). Scripture tells us that Christ "gave himself for our sins to deliver us from the present evil age" (Gal. 1:4). But Demas was deceived. Demas didn't take up the shield of faith.

The devil is a master of deception. And he's prepared to fire the missile of deception at you right now. Perhaps you are experiencing this kind of warfare in your life. You're wondering if you should even be in church. You're wondering if the Christian life is worth it. You may be questioning the veracity of the historic Christian faith. You may be questioning the orthodox teaching that you receive from your pastor. Perhaps you're rebelling against the authority of your parents. Or maybe you're shaking your fist at the authority of Scripture. The reason for this battle is spiritual in nature. The arch-enemy of your soul is firing the missile of deception - and it is hitting you right between your eyes.

Second, *notice the missile of doubt*. The devil wants us to doubt the promises of God. The enemy wants us to doubt the Word of God. And the devil wants us to doubt the character of God. This is precisely the strategy he employed with Eve.

> Did God actually say, 'You shall not eat of any tree in the garden?' (Gen. 3:1b)
>
> You will not surely die. For God knows that when you eat of it your eyes will be opened, and you will be like God, knowing good and evil. (Gen. 3:3)

Some of you are doubting the goodness of God. Others are doubting the Word of God. Some of you have been doubting God as long as you can remember. Satan will relentlessly fire the missile of doubt, hoping that you will eventually give up. His ultimate aim is for you to make shipwreck of your faith and turn away from the living God.

Finally, *consider the missile of depression*. The enemy wants to play games with our emotions. He wants to lead us into the swamp of despondence. It surprises people to learn that C.H. Spurgeon battled depression for most of his adult life. The Prince of Preachers makes this sobering lament: "My spirits were sunken so low that I could weep by the hour like a child, and yet I knew not what I wept for."[4]

King David battled bouts of depression. He writes, "Why are you cast down, O my soul, and why are you in turmoil within me?" (Ps. 43:5a).

If you are susceptible to depression, the devil will relentlessly fire his missiles at you in hopes of getting you to sink lower and lower until you either throw in the towel or are rendered powerless and ineffective.

CAPABILITY

The Bible tells us that the shield of faith gives us divine ability:

> In addition to all this, take up the shield of faith, with which you can extinguish all the flaming arrows of the evil one. (Eph. 6:16, NIV)

> In addition to all, taking up the shield of faith with which you will be able to extinguish all the flaming arrows of the evil one. (Eph. 6:16, NASB95)

Notice the word translated *can* (NIV) and *able* (NASB95). This comes from the Greek term, *dúnamai* which speaks to our ability to effectively respond to the fiery darts of the devil. The word may also be translated as power. That is, when we take up the shield of faith, God gives us divine power to extinguish the fiery darts of the devil. Extinguish means "to put out a fire or stop flames; to snuff out; to stop." Please notice that this divine ability is absolutely comprehensive. Paul says that as regenerate children of God, we have the ability to extinguish all the flaming darts of the evil one.

We have divine and supernatural ability to extinguish every accusation. We have divine and supernatural ability to extinguish every temptation. We have divine and supernatural ability to extinguish all the flaming darts of the evil one.

CONFIDENCE

When we obediently take up the shield of faith, we are filled with *confidence*. At first glance, this may not appear to be very significant, that is, until we recognize what *confidence* truly means. The word *confidence* is a compound word that contains two Latin words: *con*: "with" and *fide*: "faith." So a confident person is a person of deep faith! "Faith," writes John Piper, "is the great devil-defeater."[5] This is why Peter can confidently say, "Resist him, firm in your faith ..." (1 Pet. 5:9). Our faith and trust are in the Word of God, the promises of God, and the gospel of Jesus Christ!

If faith is the "great devil-defeater," we need to determine the best way to nurture and strengthen it. John Piper adds, "The way to thwart the devil is to strengthen the very thing he is trying most to destroy."[6]

Nurturing our faith

We nurture our faith by reading and studying the Word of God.

> Your words were found, and I ate them, and your words became to me a joy and the delight of my heart, for I am called by your name, O LORD, God of hosts. (Jer. 15:16)

We nurture our faith by meditating on the Word of God.

> I will meditate on your precepts and fix my eyes on your ways. I will delight in your statutes; I will not forget your word. (Ps. 119:15–16)

We nurture our faith by memorizing the Word of God.

> I have stored up your word in my heart, that I might not sin against you. (Ps. 119:11)

We nurture our faith by gathering together to sit under the ministry of the Word.

> And let us consider how to stir up one another to love and good works, not neglecting to meet together, as is the habit of some, but encouraging

> one another, and all the more as you see the Day drawing near. (Heb 10:24–25)

We nurture our faith by standing firm in the faith.

> Be watchful, stand firm in the faith, act like men, be strong. (1 Cor. 16:13)
>
> Not that we lord it over your faith, but we work with you for your joy, for you stand firm in your faith. (2 Cor. 1:24)
>
> By Silvanus, a faithful brother as I regard him, I have written briefly to you, exhorting and declaring that this is the true grace of God. Stand firm in it. (1 Pet. 5:12)

If you are a disciple of Jesus Christ, you possess saving faith. You will find that your faith will fluctuate. Some days your faith will be strong. Other days, it will be weak and wavering. The arch-enemy of your soul will do anything he can to weaken, marginalize, and destroy your faith. John Piper underscores this important reality: "There is no true joy without faith ... Faith is born and sustained by the Word of God, and out of faith grows the flower of joy ... Satan's number one objective is to destroy our joy of faith."[7] The polar opposite of faith is unbelief. Piper continues, "All the sinful states of our hearts are owing to unbelief in God's superabounding grace. All our sin comes from failing to be satisfied with all that God is for us in Jesus. Misplaced shame, anxiety, despondency, covetousness, lust, bitterness, impatience, pride - these all sprout from the root of unbelief in the promises of God."[8]

All this is to suggest that when we fail to believe the promises of God, we surrender the very piece of armor that God has given to protect us in on the spiritual battlefield. Therefore, may we take up the shield of faith and rest in the mighty promises of the living God.

> In all circumstances take up the shield of faith, with which you can extinguish all the flaming darts of the evil one. (Eph. 6:16)

---

1. Bonnie Berkowitz & Aaron Steckelberg, If North Korea Fires a Nuclear Weapon at the U.S., How Could it Be Stopped? (Washington Post, 29 November, 2017).
2. Ibid.
3. Ibid.
4. C.H. Spurgeon, Cited in John Piper, Future Grace (Wheaton: Crossway Books, 1995), 301.
5. John Piper, When I Don't Desire God (Wheaton: Crossway Books, 2004), 112.
6. Piper, Future Grace, 323.
7. John Piper, Desiring God (Sisters: Multnomah Books, 1996), 126, 127, 129.
8. Ibid., 323.

9

The Helmet of Salvation

... and take the helmet of salvation, and the sword of the Spirit, which is the word of God.

EPHESIANS 6:17

A POWERFUL AND PRACTICAL statement may be found in a piece of training literature for the United States Armed Forces. It says:

> Training is the Army's top priority; it prepares us to fight. As leaders, our sacred responsibility is to ensure that no soldier ever dies in combat because that soldier was not properly trained.

Likewise, Confucius reportedly said, "To lead an untrained people to war is to throw them away." The same holds true in the Christian life. Tragically, however, many Christ-followers are not properly *trained* or *equipped* to enter the battlefield. Tim Downs writes, "While Christians man the front lines in preparation for a frontal assault, the Christian worldview is being decimated by subtle, indirect guerrilla raids on our flank and rear."[1] The reason that Christian soldiers are in jeopardy is because they are not properly equipped. They have failed to take up the full armor of God.

Therefore, the need for training is great. General Eisenhower said, "From now on I am going to make it a fixed rule that no unit from the time it reaches this theater until this war is won will ever stop training."[2] Paul the apostle gives us an idea of what this training looks like in the church:

> Therefore, as you received Christ Jesus the Lord, so walk in him, rooted and built up in him and established in the faith, just as you were taught, abounding in thanksgiving. (Col. 2:6–7)

Notice several crucial observations in Paul's wartime plea. First, *we must walk in him* (Col. 2:6). The verb translated as *walk* (*peripatéō*) describes how a person conducts his life. It reveals the general character of a person. Paul uses the same term in several other New Testament passages:

- Walk in newness of life. (Rom. 6:4)
- Walk by faith, not by sight. (2 Cor. 5:7)
- Walk by the spirit. (Gal. 5:16)
- Walk in a manner worthy of the calling to which you have been called. (Eph. 4:1)

Second, *we must get firmly rooted* (Col. 2:7). *Rooted* (*rizóō*) means "to render firm or cause something to be grounded." John Calvin explains:

> For as a tree that has struck its roots deep has enough support for withstanding all the assaults

> of winds and storms, so if anyone is deeply and thoroughly fixed in Christ, as in a firm root, he cannot be thrown down from his upright position by any machinations of Satan ... If anyone has not fixed his roots in Christ, he will be carried about with every wind of doctrine, as a tree without the support is blown down at the first blast.[3]

Third, *we must get built up* (Col. 2:7). Paul uses a Greek term here that means "to finish the structure of which the foundation has already been laid; to give constant increase in Christian knowledge." We get *built up* by focusing our attention on the Word of God. We get built up by devoting our lives to doctrinal pursuits. All this leads to the fourth component in Paul's training model.

Fourth, *we must become established in the faith* (Col. 2:7). *Bebaióō* means "to make firm; to confirm; to make sure." What does training look like for the follower of Christ? We are becoming rooted, built up, and established in sound doctrine. Notice how Paul describes the walk of such a person: "For though I am absent in body, yet I am with you in spirit, rejoicing to see your good order and the firmness of your faith in Christ" (Col. 2:5).[4]

Taking up the whole armor of God has been our chief concern in part two as we have labored over Paul's charge to the Ephesian believers. We come now to the helmet of salvation.

Of course, the helmet protects the most vulnerable part of the body - the mind. It is critical that we understand how vulnerable the mind truly is. Kris Lundgaard refers to the mind as the "watchman" of our souls:

> The flesh plies deceit to knock out the watchman of your soul ... the mind is the sentinel, commanded to watch carefully over the soul by ques-

> tioning, assessing, and making judgments: Will this please God? Is this according to God's Word? If the mind determines that an action is right, the affections should then fall in line and desire, long for, and cling to that which the mind said was good and the affections hungered for. When each does its job, you obey God from the heart.[5]

Satan understands the importance of the mind. Therefore, he targets the mind and is prepared to do anything he can to infiltrate it.

The Greek term *noūs* is translated as "understanding or mind" in the New Testament. It refers to our intellect or reason in the narrower sense. The mind has the capacity for discerning spiritual truth. It is the mind, then, that recognizes good and hates evil. Scripture says:

> ... to put off your old self, which belongs to your former manner of life and is corrupt through deceitful desires, and to be renewed in the spirit of your minds (*noūs*), and to put on the new self, created after the likeness of God in true righteousness and holiness. (Eph. 4:22–24)

> For who has understood the mind of the Lord so as to instruct him? But we have the mind (*noūs*) of Christ. (1 Cor. 2:16)

> Now this I say and testify in the Lord, that you must no longer walk as the Gentiles do, in the futility of their minds (*noūs*) . (Eph. 4:17)

> And the peace of God, which surpasses all understanding, will guard your hearts and your minds (*noūs*) in Christ Jesus. (Phil. 4:7)

Another Greek term for the mind is phronéō, translated as "think or mind."

> Set your minds (*phroneîte)* on things that are above, not on things that are on earth. (Col. 3:2)
>
> Their end is destruction, their god is their belly, and they glory in their shame, with minds (*phronoûntes)* set on earthly things. But our citizenship is in heaven, and from it we await a Savior, the Lord Jesus Christ ... (Phil. 3:19–20)

And logizomai is translated as "think, reckon, count, or reason."

> Finally, brothers, whatever is true, whatever is honorable, whatever is just, whatever is pure, whatever is lovely, whatever is commendable, if there is any excellence, if there is anything worthy of praise, think (*logizesthe*) about these things. (Phil. 4:8)

Tony Evans adds, "The mind is the key to our entire being, which is why the great challenge for us today is to develop a kingdom mentality; a way of thinking that is in concert with the kingdom of which we have become a part."[6]

The enemy of our souls seeks to distract the mind. He seeks to deceive the mind. He is a master when it comes to discouraging the mind. He will distort the truth that is meant for the mind. In the end, his aim is to decimate the mind. Harry Blamires writes, "The mind of man must be won for God."[7] Notice four key areas, then, that will enable us to securely wear the helmet of salvation:

SUMMONS TO ACTION

The apostle Paul instructs Christians to "take the helmet of salvation ..." (Eph 6:17). *Take* (*déchomai*) means "to receive or accept; to take hold of." The aorist tense suggests a mindset of decisiveness. *Take* is an action word.

Paul has already described the other armor - the belt of truth, the breastplate of righteousness, the shoes of the gospel of peace, and the shield of faith. But the solider must also wear a helmet. A Roman soldier would never think about entering the battlefield without his helmet. In ancient times, the helmet was essentially a hat made of leather which was reinforced by metal. It was securely fastened to protect the most vulnerable part of the body - the head.

As followers of Jesus Christ and soldiers engaged in spiritual war, we are called upon and commanded to take up the helmet of salvation. Once the helmet is securely fastened, we are prepared for battle. We are equipped to fight.

The helmet of salvation is not only a summons to action; *it is a source of protection*.

SOURCE OF PROTECTION

The helmet of salvation protects us from at least three things. First, *it protects us from false ideas*:

> False ideas are the greatest obstacles to the reception of the gospel. We may preach with all the fervor of a reformer and yet succeed only in winning a straggler here or there, if we permit the whole collective thought of a nation or of the world to be controlled by ideas which by the resistless force of logic, prevent Christianity from being regarded as anything more than a harmless delusion.[8]

It is false ideas that the apostle Paul has in mind when he writes to the believers in Colossae: "See to it that no one takes you captive by philosophy and empty deceit, according to human tradition, according to the elemental spirits of the world, and not according to Christ" (Col. 2:8). Paul militates against any idea or philosophy that runs counter to the biblical worldview set forth in sacred Scripture. The helmet of salvation is a source of protection, guarding our minds against the pollution of a worldly system.

Second, *the helmet of salvation protects us from false "gospels."* These false "gospels" are everywhere around us. The helmet of salvation protects us from the "gospel" of humanism, the "gospel" of hedonism, and the "gospel" of works-based righteousness. And the helmet of salvation guards us against the social justice "gospel" - an idea that is being tragically promoted in churches in America and beyond. The social justice movement is largely fueled by liberal theology, which is informed by naturalism and attacks the supernatural. Theological liberalism is committed to repudiating the authority and inerrancy of Scripture and works tirelessly to discount Jesus's virgin birth, his sinless life, deity, and bodily resurrection. In short, theological liberalism is man-centered. It is the shaky and God-dishonoring foundation of the social justice movement.

Paul didn't waste any time with these erroneous ideas. He was quick to expose these man-made gospels to a church that was naive. He writes to the believers in Galatia:

> I am astonished that you are so quickly deserting him who called you in the grace of Christ and are turning to a different gospel— not that there is another one, but there are some who trouble you and want to distort the gospel of Christ. But even if we or an angel from heaven should preach to you a gospel contrary to the one we preached to you, let him be accursed. As we have said before,

> so now I say again: If anyone is preaching to you a gospel contrary to the one you received, let him be accursed. (Gal.1:6–9)

The word *gospel* means "good news. These false "gospels" are the very antithesis of good news. In the final analysis, each of these false "gospels" are damning "gospels." They look good. They appeal to our sense of accomplishment. And they build up our flesh. But Proverbs 16:25 warns, "There is a way that seems right to a man, but its end is the way to death."

Finally, *the helmet of salvation protects us from false teachers.* Paul told Timothy about two men who made shipwreck of their faith: " ... By rejecting this, some have made shipwreck of their faith, among whom are Hymenaeus and Alexander, whom I have handed over to Satan that they may learn not to blaspheme" (1 Tim. 1:19–20).

The apostle Paul warned his protege about the false teachers and he warns us as well. He refers to them as:

> Men who are puffed up with conceit and understands nothing. (1 Tim. 6:4)
>
> Men who have an unhealthy craving for controversy and quarrel about words which produce envy, dissension, slander, and evil suspicions. (1 Tim. 6:4)
>
> Men who have depraved minds and are deprived of the truth. (1 Tim. 6:5)

Paul warned Timothy about one man in particular who was peddling a false gospel (2 Tim. 4:14-16). His response to this man is reassuring and should fill our hearts with bold resolve: "But the Lord stood by me and strengthened me, so that through me the message might be fully proclaimed and all the Gentiles might hear it. So I was rescued from the lion's mouth" (2 Tim. 4:17). How could this be? Answer: the apostle Paul was wearing the helmet of salvation!

SOURCE OF POWER

Next, the helmet of salvation is a source of power. The key to tapping into this power is a transformed mind. Paul writes:

> I appeal to you therefore, brothers, by the mercies of God, to present your bodies as a living sacrifice, holy and acceptable to God, which is your spiritual worship. Do not be conformed to this world, but be transformed by the renewal of your mind, that by testing you may discern what is the will of God, what is good and acceptable and perfect. (Rom. 12:1–2)

Paul's progression for a transformed mind is clear in Romans 12:1-2 and follows a four-fold pattern. First, *we must recognize God's mercy* (v. 1). God extended mercy to us when we did not deserve it. R.C. Sproul helps us understand the critical distinction between mercy and justice: "Let us assume that all men are guilty of sin in the sight of God. From the mass of guilty humanity, God sovereignly decides to give mercy to some of them. What do the rest get? They get justice. The saved gets mercy and the unsaved get justice. Nobody gets injustice."[9] Recognizing the mercy of God should flow from a grateful heart.

Second, *we must realize the necessity of presenting our bodies as a living sacrifice to God* (v. 1). This sacrifice needs to be holy and pleasing to God. The result of such a sacrifice is an act of worship.

Third, *we must refuse to conform to the pattern of the world* (v. 2). The Greek term translated conform means "to conform ourselves (our mind and character) to another pattern," in this case, the world. Paul refers to this as the "elemental spirits of the world" (Col. 2:8).

Finally, *we must renew our minds, which results in transformation* (v. 2). Renewing our minds involves a complete renovation; a complete change for the better. Such a step is a necessary move in the direction of Christlikeness. Renew means to "cause to grow up and make new; to give new strength and vigor; to be changed into a new kind of life."[10]

SUPPORT OF TRUTH

We have seen the summons to action, the source of protection, and the source of power. Notice, finally - the support of truth. When we wear the helmet of salvation, we receive supernatural support that can be found nowhere else. Since we are in Christ, by the grace of God:[11]

- We have been justified - completely forgiven. (Rom. 5:1)
- We have died with Christ and died to the power of sin's rule over our lives. (Rom. 6:1-6)
- We are free from condemnation. (Rom. 8:1)
- We have been given the mind of Christ. (1 Cor. 2:16)
- We have been bought with a price. We are not our own. We are God's possession. (1 Cor. 6:19-20)
- We have been established, anointed, and sealed by God in Christ. (2 Cor. 1:22)
- We have died and no longer live for ourselves, but for him. (2 Cor. 5:14-15)
- We have been declared righteous. (2 Cor. 5:21)

- We have been crucified with Christ. (Gal. 2:20)
- We have been blessed with every spiritual blessing. (Eph. 1:3)
- We have been chosen in Christ before the foundation of the world to be holy and blameless in his sight. (Eph. 1:4)
- We were predestined to be adopted as a son. (Eph. 1:5)
- We have been redeemed, forgiven, and lavished with grace. (Eph. 1:7-8)
- We have been given the Holy Spirit as a deposit, which guarantees our inheritance in heaven. (Eph. 1:13-14)
- We have been made alive together with Christ. (Eph. 2:5)
- We have direct access to God through the Spirit. (Eph. 2:18)
- We may approach God with boldness, freedom, and confidence. (Eph. 3:12)
- We have been delivered from the domain of darkness and transferred to the kingdom of Christ. (Col. 1:13)
- We have been redeemed and forgiven of all our sins. (Col. 2:13-14)
- We have been raised up with Christ. (Col. 3:1-4)
- We have been saved and called according to God's doing. (2 Tim. 1:9)
- We have been reborn and renewed by the Holy Spirit. (Titus 3:5)

We have seen the indispensable need for the helmet of salvation. It is a summons to action, a source of protection, a source of power, and a support of truth. Stepping on the battlefield without a helmet is an act of foolishness. So too, in the Christian life, we must firmly secure the helmet of salvation in order to protect our minds.

If you are a follower of Christ, the helmet of salvation is an essential piece of armor that you need to wear each day. If you are not yet a Christian, today is the day of salvation. I urge you to turn from your sin and turn to the Lord Jesus Christ, trusting in his life, death on the cross, and resurrection!

> And they said, "Believe in the Lord Jesus, and you will be saved, you and your household." (Acts 16:31)

---

1. Tim Downs, Finding Common Ground (Chicago: Moody Press, 1999), 62.
2. Cited in Stephen Ambrose, D-Day (New York: Simon and Schuster, 1994), 130.
3. John Calvin, Calvin's New Testament Commentaries: XI (Grand Rapids: Eerdmans, reprint 1965), 328.
4. The NAS translates the word steréwōma as "stability." The term refers to someone who has steadfast faith, which rests upon a solid foundation. Such a person is standing as we have seen in Ephesians 6.
5. Kris Lundgaard, The Enemy Within (Phillipsburg: P&R, 1998), 55-56.

6. Tony Evans, What a Way to Live (Nashville: Word Publishing, 1997), 114.
7. Harry Blamires, The Christian Mind (Ann Arbor: Servant Publications, 1963), 81.
8. J. Gresham Machen, Cited in Charles Colson and Nancy Pearcey, How Now Shall We Live? (Wheaton: Tyndale House Publishers, 1999), 27.
9. R.C. Sproul, Chosen by God (Wheaton: Tyndale House, 1986), 37-38.
10. This term only occurs in Romans 12:2 and Titus 3:5.
11. See Neil T. Anderson and Robert L. Saucy, The Common Made Holy: Being Conformed to the Image of God (Eugene: Harvest House Publishers, 1997), 177-179.

10

The Sword of the Spirit

A holy violence, a conflict of warfare, a fight, a soldier's life, a wrestling, are spoken of as a characteristic of the true Christian.

J.C. RYLE

One of the constant messages I heard from my coaches growing up was the importance of defense. "The best offense is a good defense," they would say. I remember the championship basketball teams that Phil Jackson coached in the NBA. The mark of his teams was good defense.

We have also learned the importance of good defense in the Christian life. So far, each piece of the armor has been defensive in nature. We have seen:

- The belt of truth
- The breastplate of righteousness
- The shoes of the gospel of peace
- The shield of faith
- The helmet of salvation

The apostle Paul writes, "Therefore take up the whole armor of God, that you may be able to withstand in the evil day, and having done all, to stand firm" (Eph. 6:13). Notice the progression of Paul's thought as he tells his readers to "take the helmet of salvation, and the sword of the Spirit, which is the word of God" (Eph. 6:17). *Take* comes from the Greek word that means "to get into one's hands and take physically." We have already seen the command to "take up the helmet of salvation." In this chapter, our concern is with the sword of the Spirit.

Notice a few observations about the sword. First, *taking up the sword is not optional.* It is a command. Paul envisions a soldier who is prepared to fight. No soldier in his right mind would ever enter the battlefield without a weapon. Such an act would not only prove to be an act of foolishness; it would result in an inevitable death.

Second, *the word translated as sword comes from máxaira, "a dagger or a short sword."* This was the main weapon that the Roman soldier would use in hand-to-hand combat. And this is the same word translated as sword in Matthew 26:51.

> And behold, one of those who were with Jesus stretched out his hand and drew his sword and struck the servant of the high priest and cut off his ear.

Máxaira is used in Luke 22:49 where the disciples say to Jesus:

> And when those who were around him saw what would follow, they said, 'Lord shall we strike with the sword?'

The same word appears in Acts 12:2, which refers to Herod:

> He killed James the brother of John with the sword.

And Acts 16:27 refers to the sword as a weapon of choice:

> When the jailer woke and saw that the prison doors were open, he drew his sword and was about to kill himself, supposing that the prisoners had escaped.

Third, *taking up the sword is a strategic offensive maneuver.* While defense, as we have already seen, is important, we are also concerned with offense. This is precisely where the sword of the Spirit plays a decisive role.

Fourth, *taking up the sword is an act of obedience.* We have observed that "taking up the sword" is in the imperative mood. But notice another important exegetical insight. The verb translating *take* (*déchomai*) is written in the middle voice, which indicates that we are to "take up the sword" *by ourselves and for ourselves.* Taking up the sword is not only an act of personal obedience; it is an act that will reap great benefits in the Christian life, not to mention the battlefield!

Taken together, all these observations should cause us to see the profound importance of taking up the sword. But this isn't just any sword. Paul refers to it as the sword of the Spirit. I want you to see some of the important qualities, then, of this powerful offensive weapon.

THE CONTENT OF THE SWORD OF THE SPIRIT

The content of the Sword of the Spirit is simple, yet profound. It is the *word* (*rhēma*) *of God. Rhēma* is "a word; a saying; a statement; the content or communications or documents produced by and represented by God and his mind." This term is to be distinguished from the *word*, or the *lógos* which refers to general statements. *Rhēma* refers to individual words or particular statements. The *rhēma* of God, according to Ray Stedman, are "the sayings of God that strike home like arrows to the heart."[1]

John MacArthur adds, "The apostle is therefore not talking here about general knowledge of Scripture, but is emphasizing again the precision that comes by knowledge and understanding of specific truths."[2]

> But he answered, 'It is written, Man shall not live by bread alone, but by every word (*rhēma*) that comes from the mouth of God.' (Matt. 4:4)
>
> So faith comes from hearing, and hearing through the word (*rhēma*) of Christ. (Rom. 10:17)
>
> By faith we understand that the universe was created by the word (*rhēma*) of God, so that what is seen was not made out of things that are visible. (Heb. 11:3)

THE CHARACTERISTICS OF THE SWORD OF THE SPIRIT

The sword of the Spirit has two characteristics that we must be familiar with. First, *the sword of the Spirit is our inerrant authority*. "The inerrancy of Scripture means that the Scripture in the original manuscripts does not affirm anything that is contrary to fact."[3] Therefore, we bank on the truthfulness of Scripture.

Second, *the sword of the Spirit is our final authority*. Wayne Grudem adds, "The authority of Scripture means that all the words of Scripture are God's words in such a way that to disbelieve or disobey any word of Scripture is to disbelieve or disobey God."[4]

> All Scripture is breathed out by God and profitable for teaching, for reproof, for correction, and for training in righteousness ... (2 Tim. 3:16)
>
> For no prophecy was ever produced by the will of man, but men spoke from God as they were carried along by the Holy Spirit. (2 Pet.1:21)

Therefore, we don't trifle with God's Word. We don't marginsalize or compromise God's Word. We don't play games with sacred Scripture. The sword of the Spirit is our highest authority.

The authority of Scripture is grounded on the immutability of God. Indeed, God does not change (Mal. 3:6; Heb. 6:17-18). God is consistent in truth. (Jer. 10:10; Exod. 34:6; Deut. 32:4; 1 John 5:20). God will never contradict himself. Therefore, the Bible must be our highest authority.[5] *The Westminster Confession of Faith* continues:

> The whole counsel of God, concerning all things necessary for his own glory, man's salvation, faith, and life, is either expressly set down in Scripture, or by good and necessary consequence may be deduced from Scripture; unto which nothing at any time is to be added, whether by new revelations of the Spirit or traditions of men.[6]

And Francis Schaeffer provides this fitting summary:

> It is my conviction that the crucial area of discussion for evangelicalism in the next years will be the Scripture. At stake is whether evangelicalism will remain evangelical ... We must say that if evangelicals are to be evangelicals, we must not compromise our view of Scripture ... Holding to a strong view of Scripture or not holding to it is the watershed of the evangelical world.[7]

THE CONQUERING POWER OF THE SWORD OF THE SPIRIT

The sword of the Spirit provides conquering power in the Christian life. The sword is the divine instrument that the Spirit uses to accomplish several important tasks. First, *the sword of the Spirit instructs, edifies, and encourages us.*

> And now I commend you to God and to the word of his grace, which is able to build you up and to give you the inheritance among all those who are sanctified. (Acts 20:32)

> For whatever was written in former days was written for our instruction, that through endurance and through the encouragement of the Scriptures we might have hope. (Rom. 15:4)

> Therefore, as you received Christ Jesus the Lord, so walk in him, rooted and built up in him and established in the faith, just as you were taught, abounding in thanksgiving. (Col. 2:6–7)

Second, *the sword of the Spirit strengthens us.*

> Like newborn infants, long for the pure spiritual milk, that by it you may grow up into salvation. (1 Pet. 2:2)

The sword of the Spirit is the divine means that God has chosen to use in the lives of his people to mature the people of God.

Third, *the sword of the Spirit convicts us.* Jesus refers to the Spirit as the "Spirit of truth" (John 14:17).

> And when he comes, he will convict the world concerning sin and righteousness and judgment. (John 16:8).

Fourth, *the sword of the spirit helps us battle temptation.*

> The devil said to him, 'If you are the Son of God, command this stone to become bread.' And Jesus answered him, 'It is written, 'Man shall not live by bread alone.' And the devil took him up and showed him all the kingdoms of the world in a moment of time, and said to him, 'To you I will give all this authority and their glory, for it has been delivered to me, and I give it to whom I will. If you, then, will worship me, it will all be yours.' And Jesus answered him, 'It is written,' 'You shall worship the Lord your God, and him only shall you serve.' And he took him to Jerusalem and set him on the pinnacle of the temple and said to him, 'If you are the Son of God, throw yourself down from here, for it is written,' 'He will command his angels concerning you, to guard you,' and 'On their hands they will bear you up, lest you strike your foot against a stone.' " And Jesus

> answered him, 'It is said, 'You shall not put the Lord your God to the test.' And when the devil had ended every temptation, he departed from him until an opportune time. (Luke 4:3–13)

Fifth, *the sword of the Spirit brings us joy.*

> Blessed is the man who walks not in the counsel of the wicked, nor stands in the way of sinners, nor sits in the seat of scoffers; but his delight is in the law of the LORD, and on his law he meditates day and night. (Ps. 1:1–2)
>
> But he said, "Blessed rather are those who hear the word of God and keep it! (Luke 11:28)

Finally, *the sword of the Spirit regenerates the spiritually dead.*

> ...he saved us, not because of works done by us in righteousness, but according to his own mercy, by the washing of regeneration and renewal of the Holy Spirit. (Titus 3:5)
>
> So faith comes from hearing, and hearing through the word of Christ." (Rom. 10:17)

The Word of God accomplishes each of these things with great effectiveness. " ... so shall my word be that goes out from my mouth; it shall not return to me empty, but it shall accomplish that which I purpose, and shall succeed in the thing for which I sent it" (Isa. 55:11). The Spirit of God uses the Word of God to transform the people of God. This is the conquering power of the sword of the Spirit.

When you fail to take up the sword of the Spirit, you forfeit spiritual power. When you fail to take up the sword of the Spirit, you forfeit spiritual authority. When you fail to take up the sword of the Spirit, you forfeit encouragement and edification. When you fail to take up the sword of the Spirit, you invite defeat.

You are engaged in a daily war against sin. May you be a man or woman of the Book. May the Word of God inform all your decisions. May the Word of God expose every error. May the Word of God guide your steps on the narrow path that leads to the Celestial City. And may you wield the mighty sword of the Spirit to the praise and honor of God!

> Let the word of Christ dwell in you richly, teaching and admonishing one another in all wisdom, singing psalms and hymns and spiritual songs, with thankfulness in your hearts to God. (Col. 3:16)

---

1. Ray Stedman, Spiritual Warfare, 116.

2. John MacArthur, Ephesians (Chicago: Moody Press, 1986), 370.
3. Wayne Grudem, Systematic Theology (Grand Rapids: Zondervan, 1994), 90.
4. Ibid., 73.
5. Adapted from Ron Carlson, Unpublished class notes.
6. G.I. Williamson, The Westminster Confession of Faith (Philadelphia: P&R Publishing, 1964), 9.
7. Francis A. Schaeffer, No Final Conflict (Wheaton: Crossway Books, 1982), 119, 121-122.

11

Prayer

Give yourself to prayer, to reading and meditation on divine truths: strive to penetrate to the bottom of them and never be content with a superficial knowledge.

DAVID BRAINERD

In our fallen world, we struggle with disaster, doubt, discouragement, and depression. Each of us face a culture which is plagued by spiritual darkness. This spiritual darkness, along with every form of sin will one day be vanquished by the Lord Jesus Christ. So we wait patiently for Jesus to make all things new, where righteousness will dwell on the New Earth. Until that day, we will continue to struggle. We will continue to inch forward.

We have learned that we are in a battle. The battle is intense. And the battle is spiritual in nature. Ephesians 6:12 says, "For we do not wrestle against flesh and blood, but against the rulers, against the authorities, against the cosmic powers over this present darkness, against the spiritual forces of evil in the heavenly places."

We have also learned about the importance of maintaining spiritual courage. Paul writes, "Finally, be strong in the Lord and in the strength of his might" (Eph. 6:10). Scripture commands us to be courageous. This courage is centered on the Lord Jesus Christ. While conventional wisdom tells us to take matters into our own hands and rely on our own abilities, resources, intelligence, and ingenuity, Scripture calls us to a higher path. We must "be strong in the Lord and in the strength of his might."

God not only requires *divine courage*; he requires *divine enablement*. We are granted both as we put on the whole armor of God, which includes the belt of truth, the breastplate of righteousness, the shoes of the gospel of peace, the shield of faith, the helmet of salvation, and as we take up the sword of the Spirit.

Faithful followers of Christ will eagerly and obediently put on the full armor of God, which will protect us and equip our hands for battle. But Paul is not done. He adds one additional element, which proves to be a mighty source of strength on the battlefield. He includes an additional weapon - one that is to be used in tandem with the sword of the Spirit. The apostle concludes his letter to the church in Ephesus with these penetrating words:

> ... praying at all times in the Spirit, with all prayer and supplication. To that end, keep alert with all perseverance, making supplication for all the saints, and also for me, that words may be given to me in opening my mouth boldly to proclaim the mystery of the gospel, for which I am an ambassador in chains, that I may declare it boldly, as I ought to speak. So that you also may know how I am and what I am doing, Tychicus the beloved brother and faithful minister in the Lord will tell you everything. I have sent him to you for this very purpose, that you may know how we are, and that he may encourage your hearts. Peace be to the brothers, and love with faith, from God the Father and the Lord Jesus Christ. (Eph. 6:18–23)

Saints through the ages have stressed the importance of prayer:

> Prayer is a sincere, sensible, affectionate pouring out of the heart or soul to God, through Christ, in the strength and assistance of the Holy Spirit, for such things as God has promised, or according to his Word, for the good of the church, with submission in faith to the will of God.[1]

> Prayer is that point in religion at which you must be most of all on your guard. Here it is that true religion begins; here it flourishes, and here it decays. Tell me what a man's prayers are, and I will soon tell you the state of his soul. Prayer is the spiritual pulse. By this the spiritual health may be tested. Prayer is the spiritual weatherglass. By this we may know whether it is fair or foul with our hearts.[2]

THE MEANING OF PRAYER

Praying comes from the Greek term, *proseúchomai* which means "to pay attention; to hold a ship in a direction." It means to "attend to" or "give attention to something" - in this case, God. One might say, then, that prayer is focused and attentive communication with the living God.

Martin Luther established a reputation as a mighty man of prayer. In the preface to his *Larger Catechism*, he writes:

> We know that our defense lies in prayer alone. We are too weak to resist the devil and his vassals. Let us hold fast to the weapons of the Christian; they enable us to combat the devil. For what has carried off these great victories over the undertak-

> ings of our enemies which the devil has used to put us in subjection, if not the prayers of certain pious people who rose up as a rampart to protect us.[3]

Luther continues, "Our enemies may mock us. But we shall oppose both men and the devil if we maintain ourselves in prayer and if we persist in it. For we know that when a Christian prays in this way: 'Dear Father, Your will be done,' God replies to him, 'Dear child, yes, it shall be done in spite of the devil and the whole world.'"[4]

Since Luther had a reputation for being a man of prayer, his barber Peter Beskendorf, known as the "Master Barber," asked Luther to teach him how to pray. Luther responded by writing a 34-page book, which he dedicated to his friend: "As a shoemaker makes a shoe, and a tailor makes a coat, so ought a Christian to pray. Prayer is the daily business of a Christian."

Luther taught Master Barber how to pray by following the pattern of *The Lord's Prayer*. The first petition in the prayer is well-known: "Hallowed be Your name." Luther prays:

> Yes, Lord God, dear Father, hallowed be Your name, both in us and throughout the whole world. Destroy and root out the abominations, idolatry, and heresy of all false teachers and fanatics who wrongly use Your name and in scandalous ways take it in vain and horribly blaspheme it. They instantly boast that they teach Your Word and the laws of the church, though they really use the devil's deceit and trickery in Your name to wretchedly seduce many poor souls throughout the world, even killing and shedding much innocent blood, and in such persecution, they believe that they render You a divine service.

> Dear Lord God, convert and restrain them. Convert those who are still to be converted that they with us and we with them may hallow and praise Your name, both with true and pure doctrine and with a good and holy life. Restrain those who are unwilling to be converted so that they be forced to cease from misusing, defiling, and dishonoring Your holy name and from misleading the poor people. Amen.[5]

THE MANDATE OF PRAYER

The mandate to pray is clear and unmistakable. First, *prayer is assumed*. It is interesting that Paul does not use the imperative mood as he relays the importance of prayer to the Christ-followers in Ephesus. The command to pray is certainly an important theme in Scripture:

> But I say to you, Love your enemies and pray for those who persecute you. (Matt. 5:44)
>
> Pray then like this: "Our Father in heaven, hallowed be your name. (Matt. 6:9)
>
> ... Pray earnestly to the Lord of the harvest to send out laborers into his harvest. (Matt. 9:38)
>
> Watch and pray that you may not enter into temptation. The spirit indeed is willing, but the flesh is weak. (Matt. 26:41)
>
> ...Pray without ceasing. (1 Thess. 5:17)
>
> Brothers, pray for us. (1 Thess. 5:25)

> Is anyone among you suffering? Let him pray. Is anyone cheerful? Let him sing praise. (Jas. 5:13)

> Therefore, confess your sins to one another and pray for one another, that you may be healed. The prayer of a righteous person has great power as it is working. (Jas. 5:16)

Paul assumes that the Christians in Ephesus will pray. He assumes that you and I will pray - for it is a normal part of living the Christian life. "God expects us to use the walkie-talkie of prayer because that is the means He has ordained not only for godliness, but also for the spiritual warfare between His kingdom and the kingdom of His enemy. To abandon prayer is to fight the battle with our own resources at best, and to lose interest in the battle at worst."[6] Therefore, we commit ourselves to prayer on the battlefield.

Second, *prayer is ongoing. Proseúchomai* is a present tense verb in Ephesians 6:18 that could be translated as "praying continuously" or "praying as a matter of habit." This pattern of prayer should not surprise us - it is a pattern we see over and over in the Bible:

> Rejoice in hope, be patient in tribulation, be constant in prayer. (Rom. 12:12)

> ... Pray without ceasing. (1 Thess. 5:17)

> For God is my witness, whom I serve with my spirit in the gospel of his Son, that without ceasing I mention you always in my prayers, asking that somehow by God's will I may now at last succeed in coming to you. (Rom. 1:9–10)

> I give thanks to my God always for you because

> of the grace of God that was given you in Christ Jesus. (1 Cor. 1:4)
>
> Continue steadfastly in prayer, being watchful in it with thanksgiving. (Col. 4:2)
>
> As we pray most earnestly night and day that we may see you face to face and supply what is lacking in your faith? (1 Thess. 3:10)
>
> To this end we always pray for you, that our God may make you worthy of his calling and may fulfill every resolve for good and every work of faith by his power ... (2 Thess. 1:11)
>
> I thank God whom I serve, as did my ancestors, with a clear conscience, as I remember you constantly in my prayers night and day. (2 Tim. 1:3)

Third, *prayer is in the Spirit*. Prayer in the Spirit is not some kind of subjective experience. Nor does it have anything to do with charismatic expression. Listen to John MacArthur's explanation:

> To pray in the Spirit is to pray in the name of Christ, to pray consistent with His nature and will. To pray in the Spirit is to pray in concert with the Spirit, who 'helps our weaknesses; for we do not know how to pray as we should, but the Spirit himself intercedes for us with groaning too deep for words; and He who searches the hearts knows what the mind of the Spirit is, because he intercedes for the saints according to the will of God.' (Rom 8:26-27)[7]

Prayer in the Spirit is placing proper reliance on the third member of the Trinity, acknowledging his power and presence in our lives.

Finally, *prayer is an urgent request*. The apostle Paul writes, " ... praying at all times in the Spirit, with all prayer and supplication" (Eph. 6:18). The Greek term translated *supplication* is also translated as prayer:

> Brothers, my heart's desire and prayer to God for them is that they may be saved. (Rom. 10:1)
>
> Always in every prayer of mine for you all making my prayer with joy. (Phil. 1:4)
>
> Therefore, confess your sins to one another and pray for one another, that you may be healed. The prayer of a righteous person has great power as it is working. (Jas. 5:16)

But the term translated as *prayer* in Ephesians 6:18 is more than a mere prayer request as one might expect. It has an urgency attached to it. This is a word that implies an entreaty. Scripture encourages us to pray like this:

> And the Lord's servant must not be quarrelsome but kind to everyone, able to teach, patiently enduring evil, correcting his opponents with gentleness. God may perhaps grant them repentance leading to a knowledge of the truth, and they may come to their senses and escape from the snare of the devil, after being captured by him to do his will. (2 Tim. 2:24–26)
>
> Do not be anxious about anything, but in every-

> thing by prayer and supplication with thanksgiving let your requests be made known to God. (Phil. 4:6)

So cry out to the Lord. He hears your prayers. He hears your requests and supplications. "The only way to come to God," writes Paul Miller, "is by taking off any spiritual mask. The real you has to meet the real God. He is a person. So instead of being frozen by your self-protection, talk with God about your worries ... Don't be embarrassed by how needy your heart is and how much it needs to cry out for grace. Just start praying."[8] Tell God about your needs. Tell him about your frustrations and longings. Talk to him about your battle with temptation. Acknowledge the sin you are wrestling with. Run to him with your every request. And may the words of Scripture strengthen your resolve: "Let us then with confidence draw near to the throne of grace, that we may receive mercy and find grace to help in time of need" (Heb. 4:16).

In the film *Gladiator*, Russell Crow plays Maximus Decimus Meridius, a Roman soldier who is sent to the forest to be executed but manages to escape. He stands face-to-face with his interrogator who attempts to wield his sword in the frigid cold air. Maximus says with an icy stare, "The frost. Sometimes it makes the blade stick!" This scene is a vivid reminder for followers of Jesus Christ. We must remain vigilant. We must constantly be on guard.

Jonathan Edwards challenges us in this regard: "Seeing we have such a prayer-hearing God as we have heard, let us be much employed in the duty of prayer: let us pray with all prayer and supplication: let us live prayerful lives, continuing instant in prayer, watching thereunto with all perseverance; praying always, without ceasing, earnestly, and not fainting."[9] Paul concludes his letter to the Ephesians with these stirring words:

> So that you also may know how I am and what I am doing, Tychicus the beloved brother and faithful minister in the Lord will tell you everything. I have sent him to you for this very purpose, that you may know how we are, and that he may encourage your hearts. Peace be to the brothers, and love with faith, from God the Father and the Lord Jesus Christ. Grace be with all who love our Lord Jesus Christ with love incorruptible. (Eph. 6:21–24)

Oh, dear reader. May you pay heed to Paul's plea to pray. Be much on your knees in prayer. May God find you faithful in your battle against sin!

---

1. John Bunyan, Prayer (Edinburgh: Banner of Truth, reprint 1662), 13.
2. J.C. Ryle, A Call to Prayer (Edinburgh: Banner of Truth, 2002), 32.
3. Martin Luther, Cited in A Simple Way to Pray, Loc. 385.
4. Ibid.
5. Ibid., Loc. 385-540.
6. Donald S. Whitney, Spiritual Disciplines for the Christian Life (Colorado Springs: NavPress, 1991), 83.
7. John F. MacArthur, Ephesians (Chicago: Moody Press, 1986), 380.
8. Paul Miller, A Praying Life.
9. Jonathan Edwards, The Most High and Prayer Hearing God.

PART III: THE PLAN TO DEFEAT SIN

"AND THE LORD GOD commanded the man, saying, 'You may surely eat of every tree of the garden, but of the tree of the knowledge of good and evil you shall not eat, for in the day that you eat of it you shall surely die'" (Gen. 2:16–17). We have seen the violation of that critical command and the horrible death march which has ensued ever since that day.

When God makes a promise, he intends to keep it. So when Adam and Eve disobeyed, they began a long journey that led to death: "Therefore, just as sin came into the world through one man, and death through sin, and so death spread to all men because all sinned" (Rom. 5:12). Paul continues to unfold the devastating consequences of sin in Romans 5:14. He writes, "Yet death reigned from Adam to Moses, even over those whose sinning was not like the transgression of Adam, who was a type of the one who was to come."

Tragically, some Christians either don't understand the importance of battling sin or have chosen to disregard its pernicious influence in their lives. J.C. Ryle warns, "Oh, let not the devil succeed in persuading you that sin is a small matter!"[1]

Sun Tzu said: "The art of war is of vital importance to the State. It is a matter of life and death, a road either to safety or to ruin. Hence it is a subject of inquiry which can on no account be neglected."[2] The great Chinese strategist continues, "If you know the enemy and know yourself, you need not fear the result of a hundred battles. If you know yourself but not the enemy, for every victory gained you will suffer a defeat. If you know neither the enemy nor yourself, you will succumb in every battle."[3]

In part three, we will discover the biblical plan to defeat sin. Does the plan for defeating sin involve relying on God and the grace he sovereignly supplies? Does the plan for defeating sin involve our responsible participation? The answer is a resounding "yes." That is, we have a responsibility to defeat sin, but only in the strength that God supplies. The Christian life, then, is a matter of both passive trust and active obedience. Sin is not the end of the story. Jesus the Conqueror has defeated sin. Jesus has not only defeated the power of sin; he has also defeated sin's penalty. And one day, this Conqueror will eradicate sin's very presence.

---

1. J.C. Ryle, Thoughts for Young Men (Louisville: GLH Publishing, 2017), Loc. 379.
2. Sun Tzu, The Art of War (New York: Barnes and Noble Classics, 2003), 7.
3. Ibid., 17.

12

The Reign of Grace

He saved us, not because of works done by us in righteousness, but according to his own mercy, by the washing of regeneration and renewal of the Holy Spirit.

TITUS 3:5

John Newton was born in London, England (1725). Newton became a sailor and a slave-trading captain. He lived a reckless life of sin and debauchery until he was rescued and regenerated by the grace of God in Christ and later became a pastor. The one who enslaved the image-bearers of God and was a slave to sin himself became a slave of the living God!

What do we have in common with John Newton? Some may originate from London. Others may fancy themselves a sailor. My guess is none of us could, in good conscience, include slave trader on our resumes. However, we will learn that each of us actually share some common qualities with the former British slave trader.

One of the mighty truths that Newton learned was this: "I am a great sinner and Christ is a great Savior." Indeed, the greatest need of every sinner is the free gift of salvation, which is found in Christ alone. In order to appreciate this great need, we must see the reign of grace in the soul of man. Notice three important headings:

- The Reign of Sin
- The Remarkable Appearance of Christ
- The Reign of Grace

THE REIGN OF SIN

In whom does sin reign?

Sin reigns with unrelenting force in every unconverted person. Each person is born with a sinful nature. "Behold, I was brought forth in iniquity," says David, "and in sin did my mother conceive me" (Ps. 51:5). Sin is comprehensive in scope. It affects all people. Nobody can escape the horrible clutches of sin's reach. Paul the apostle spells out the devastating news: "Therefore, just as sin came into the world through one man, and death through sin, and so death spread to all men because all sinned" (Rom. 5:12). "For all have sinned and fall short of the glory of God" (Rom. 3:23).

What is the nature of sin's reign?

Sin is a brutal task-master. Left to itself, sin will dominate our lives. Sin left unchecked will rule and reign with a force that can never be tamed. Scripture reveals the end result of sinners who refuse to submit to God:

> And since they did not see fit to acknowledge God, God gave them up to a debased mind to do what ought not to be done. They were filled with all manner of unrighteousness, evil, covetousness, malice. They are full of envy, murder, strife, deceit, maliciousness. They are gossips, slander-

> ers, haters of God, insolent, haughty, boastful, inventors of evil, disobedient to parents, foolish, faithless, heartless, ruthless. Though they know God's righteous decree that those who practice such things deserve to die, they not only do them but give approval to those who practice them. (Rom. 1:28–32)

In Jeremiah 17:9, the prophet laments, "The heart is deceitful above all things, and desperately sick; who can understand it?" And Paul notes that unchecked sin reigns in death (Rom. 5:21).

When does sin reign?

Sin reigned before we were rescued and redeemed by the Lord Jesus Christ. Romans 5:18-21 outlines how our lives in Adam were dominated by sin. Paul argues that "one trespass led to condemnation for all men" (v. 18). Through Adam's disobedience, many were made sinners (v. 19). The law came to increase the trespass (v. 20). And "sin reigned in death" (v. 21). *Reign* comes from the Greek term, *basileúō,* which means "to reign as king; to control completely." Before grace, we were totally dominated by sin. Before the Holy Spirit regenerated our hearts and gave us the ability to believe the gospel, our lives were under sin's spell. Our actions, attitudes, motives, and wills were held captive by the reign of sin.

What is the reality of life apart from grace?

Titus 3:3 reveals the reality of life apart from grace: "For we ourselves were once foolish, disobedient, led astray, slaves to various passions and pleasures, passing our days in malice and envy, hated by others and hating one another" (Titus 3:3). Where grace is absent, sin runs its course and dominates the unsuspecting.

John Newton understood the unfathomable depth of his sin. He writes, "By nature how depraved, how prone to every ill, (their) lives to Satan how enslaved, how obstinate (their) will."[1]

If you have not yet trusted in Christ and banked all your hope on his life, death, burial, and resurrection - you are still under the reign of sin. The trajectory of your life is heading hopelessly for hell. The good news is that when you come to terms with the reign of sin in your life, you are prepared to come face-to-face with the remarkable appearance of Christ.

THE REMARKABLE APPEARANCE OF CHRIST

In Titus 3:3 the apostle Paul marks a sharp contrast between the hopelessness that unconverted people experience with a *but* that appears in the next verse: "But when the goodness and loving kindness of God our Savior appeared ..." (Titus 3:4). This is the greatest news that sinners could ever imagine!

What is the meaning of this appearance?

The Bible says that God *appeared* (*èpiphaínō*), a word that means "to publish; to present oneself formally; to be manifested; to make one known to the world." Titus 2:13 points to the appearance of Christ: "... waiting for our blessed hope, the appearing of the glory of our great God and Savior Jesus Christ." The same term also appears in Luke 1:79: " ... to give light (*èpiphaínō*) to those who sit in darkness and in the shadow of death, to guide our feet into the way of peace" (Luke 1:79).

Who is this God who appeared?

The appearance of the Savior is the most important event in human history. No appearance has been more greatly anticipated than the revelation of Jesus Christ. He is the one that Matthew revealed, would "save his people from their sins" (Matt. 1:21). He is a God who demonstrates goodness (Titus 3:4). He is our Savior - and his name is Jesus Christ!

What if God had never appeared?

If God never appeared, we would be dominated by the tyranny of sin. We would be decimated by sin's brutal dictatorship. We would not know real joy. We would fail to understand real life.

We would not enjoy eternal life. We would all go to hell! So, the appearance of God is good news for those who are currently deposed by sin's cruel reign.

THE REIGN OF GRACE

We have witnessed the reign of sin. We have seen the remarkable appearance of Christ. Finally, notice the reign of grace.

Christ appeared in order to save us

Titus 3:5 says, "He saved us, not because of works done by us in righteousness, but according to his own mercy, by the washing of regeneration and renewal of the Holy Spirit." The phrase, he saved us means "to deliver or rescue." Each sinner needs to be rescued from the penalty of sin, the power of sin, and the presence of sin. "For the Son of Man came to seek and to save the lost" (Luke 19:10). He saved us from our sins, that is, Jesus forgives sinners:

> ... for this is my blood of the covenant, which is poured out for many for the forgiveness of sins. (Matt. 26:28)

> He has delivered us from the domain of darkness and transferred us to the kingdom of his beloved Son, in whom we have redemption, the forgiveness of sins. (Col. 1:13-14)

> Blessed are those whose lawless deeds are forgiven, and whose sins are covered. (Rom. 4:7)

> She will bear a son, and you shall call his name Jesus, for he will save his people from their sins. (Matt. 1:21)

He saved us from the wrath of God:

> Since, therefore, we have now been justified by his blood, much more shall we be saved by him from the wrath of God. (Rom. 5:9)
>
> Whoever believes in the Son has eternal life; whoever does not obey the Son shall not see life, but the wrath of God remains on him. (John 3:36)

The basis of salvation is the mercy of God

God is a good God who delights in showering his people with lovingkindness. Indeed, he is a merciful God who expresses his great love for us on the cross of Christ. *Mercy* (*Éleos*) is God's compassion and faithfulness toward the people of God. It is specifically defined as "that divine quality by which God faithfully keeps his promises and maintains his covenant relationship despite his people's unworthiness/unfaithfulness." Ephesians 2:4 tells us that God is rich in mercy. And Peter describes it in vivid terms: "Blessed be the God and Father of our Lord Jesus Christ! According to his great mercy, he has caused us to be born again to a living hope through the resurrection of Jesus Christ from the dead" (1 Pet. 1:3).

Salvation is not by works -- He did what sinful people could never do for themselves. "We have all become like one who is unclean, and all our righteous deeds are like a polluted garment. We all fade like a leaf, and our iniquities, like the wind, take us away" (Isa. 64:6). You need to understand that you can never earn your way to heaven. You can never achieve right standing with God on your own (attending church, doing good things, getting baptized, tithing, doing ministry, not doing "bad" things, etc).

In the final analysis, you need to stand on the merits of Another, namely, the Lord Jesus Christ who died in your place. C.H. Spurgeon adds, "Works of righteousness are the fruit of salvation, and the root must come before the fruit. The Lord saves His people out of clear, unmixed, undiluted mercy and grace, and for no other reason."

The means of grace through which we are saved is regeneration and renewal of the Holy Spirit

First, *regeneration is the sovereign act of the Holy Spirit, which awakens dead and unresponsive sinners and changes the desires of their hearts which grants them the ability to believe the gospel.*

J.I. Packer defines regeneration as:

> the spiritual change wrought in the heart of man by the Holy Spirit in which his/her inherently sinful nature is changed so that he/she can respond to God in faith, and live in accordance with His will (John 3:3,5 7; Tit. 3:5). It extends to the whole nature of man, altering his governing disposition, illuminating his mind, freeing his will, and renewing his nature.[2]

R.C. Sproul clearly articulates the truth of regeneration:

> The Spirit recreates the human heart, quickening it from spiritual death to spiritual life. Regenerate people are new creations. Where formerly they had no disposition, inclination, or desire for the things of God, now they are disposed and inclined toward God. In regeneration, God plants a desire for Himself in the human heart that otherwise would not be there.[3]

We get a glimpse of this special work in the Old Testament. "And the Lord your God will circumcise your heart and the heart of your offspring, so that you will love the Lord your God with all your heart and with all your soul, that you may live" (Deut. 30:6). And Ezekiel 36:26 describes the miracle of regeneration: "And I will give you a new heart, and a new spirit I will put within you. And I will remove the heart of stone from your flesh and give you a heart of flesh."

Second, *regeneration is the sovereign work of God* (John 3:3-8). Jesus makes this emphatic point in John 6:63. He says, "It is the Spirit who gives life; the flesh is no help at all. The words that I have spoken to you are spirit and life." And Paul clearly describes the sovereignty of God in salvation: "So then he has mercy on whomever he wills, and he hardens whomever he wills" (Rom. 9:18).[4]

Third, *regeneration is the miraculous work of God. When the Holy Spirit regenerates your heart, everything changes.* Your desires change, your will is freed, your nature is renewed. You become a new person! (See Ezek. 36:26; Jer. 31:31-34).

Finally, *regeneration is the sole work of God.* Sinners are utterly passive in regeneration. That is, there is no human participation. "Regeneration," writes Loraine Boettner, "is something which is wrought in us, and not an act performed by us."[5] Scripture clearly proclaims monergistic regeneration. That is, God alone transforms the darkened, hardened heart of a sinner into one that is alive to God: "Blessed be the God and Father of our Lord Jesus Christ! According to his great mercy, he has caused us to be born again to a living hope through the resurrection of Jesus Christ from the dead" (1 Pet. 1:3).

And the apostle John drives home the amazing reality of monergistic regeneration as well: "But to all who did receive him, who believed in his name, he gave the right to become children of God, who were born, not of blood nor of the will of the flesh nor of the will of man, but of God" (John 1:12-13).

But not everyone is happy to confess the sovereign role of the Spirit in regeneration. Some Semi-Pelagian sympathizers are eager to attribute a measure of credit to the human will. Instead of embracing the biblical truth of monergism, they hold to synergism which maintains that the sinner cooperates with the Holy Spirit in order for regeneration to take place. This is usually expressed in doctrinal statements and sermons by pleading with unconverted people to "believe" in order to be born again. But Jesus does not tell Nicodemus believe in order to be born again. He simply says, "Truly, truly, I say to you, unless one is born again he cannot see the kingdom of God" (John 3:3). Jesus continues, "Truly, truly, I say to you, unless one is born of water and the Spirit, he cannot enter the kingdom of God. That which is born of the flesh is flesh, and that which is born of the Spirit is spirit. Do not marvel that I said to you, 'You must be born again'" (John 3:5-7).

Several years ago, I attended a denominational forum that was discussing the modification of our doctrinal statement. When we debated the subject of monergistic regeneration, one pastor was especially animated. He defended free will by zealously citing John 1:12. "But to all who did receive him, who believed in his name, he gave the right to become children of God." Silence filled the room of over one hundred pastors. I raised my hand and gently posed a question: "What do you do with verse 13?" I asked. The pastor lowered his eyes and gazed at his Bible as he silently read the text: "... Who were born, not of blood nor of the will of the flesh nor of the will of man, but of God" His response was chilling: "Well, I guess I never noticed that verse before." The momentary silence was deafening as this man quickly realized that his exegesis had been conveniently eclipsed by his erroneous doctrinal presuppositions.

I do not retell this story to belittle a fellow pastor in any way. My intent is to show the subtle ways that Semi-Pelagianism has crept into the fabric of the church. The zealous man who defended synergism had obviously been duped into embracing a version of libertarian free will that is simply not found in

Scripture. Instead of clinging to the truth of monergistic regeneration, he clung to the Arminian understanding of free will which guided his understanding of Scripture.

Jesus slices through the theological fog by describing the exclusive role of the Holy Spirit in granting spiritual life to sinners who are dead in trespasses and sins: "It is the Spirit who gives life; the flesh is no help at all. The words that I have spoken to you are spirit and life" (John 6:63).

Christ appeared to save us. This is the reign of grace. When God's grace captures your heart, your life changes. This does not mean that temptation goes away. But it does mean that the inclination of your heart changes. When God's grace reigns in our souls, we are victorious. When grace reigns in our souls, we are delivered from the penalty of sin. When grace reigns in our souls, we are delivered from the power of sin.

This change is all-encompassing and radical. Instead of pursuing foolish things, we pursue a life of wisdom. While we were once led astray, we now have direction and begin pursuing God's plan for our lives. While we were once consumed with malice and envy, we now demonstrate a supernatural love for people. Instead of pursuing the passions and pleasures of the world, we pursue the pleasures of Christ! Instead of following after the petty pleasures of materialism, we find our joy in God. Indeed, "the pursuit of joy in God is not only innocent, it is essential. The birth of that pursuit is the birth of the Christian life."[6]

The greatest need of every sinner is salvation. We have seen the reign of sin, which is the essence of our problem. We have learned that sin unchecked will destroy our lives. The reality is this: life apart from God is hell on earth.

But we have also seen the remarkable appearance of Christ and the reign of grace. Christ's appearance and the salvation he offers is wrapped up in one word: grace. Martin Lloyd Jones says, "The Christian life starts with grace, it must continue with grace, it must end with grace."

John Newton knew the reality of sin's reign as a slave trader. He came face-to-face with the appearance of God as he was confronted with the light of the gospel. He understood the reign of grace in the soul of man. And he understood that the greatest need of every sinner is salvation. His epitaph reads:

> JOHN NEWTON, Clerk, once an infidel and Libertine, a Servant of Slaves in Africa, was, by the rich mercy of our Lord and Savior, Jesus Christ, preserved, restored, pardoned, and appointed to preach the faith he had long labored to destroy.

What do you have in common with John Newton? Each one of us has the heart of a slave-trader beating within us. Each one of us is born into this world as an infidel and a God-hater. Each of us has an inbred antipathy for God.

Newton's heart was conquered by grace. Grace reigned in his soul. "Now the law came in to increase the trespass, but where sin increased, grace abounded all the more, so that, as sin reigned in death, grace also might reign through righteousness leading to eternal life through Jesus Christ our Lord." (Rom. 5:20–21). Here's the bottom line: Either sin reigns or grace reigns. Is grace reigning in your soul?

---

1. John Newton, Cited in John F. MacArthur, Slave: The Hidden Truth About Your Identity in Christ (Nashville: Thomas Nelson, 2012), 111.
2. J.I. Packer, Regeneration (www.monergism.com), 2005.
3. R.C. Sproul, Essential Truths of the Christian Faith (Wheaton: Tyndale Publishers, 1998), 171-172.
4. The Holy Spirit regenerates the elect monergistically. Human effort and human response play no role at the point of regeneration.
5. Loraine Boettner, The Reformed Doctrine of Predestination, 165.
6. John Piper, Desiring God, 69.

13

Establishing Settled Convictions

Since we are kings, it becomes us to fight manfully against sin, the world, and the devil, that we may reign with Christ.

ZACHARIUS URSINUS

THE BATTLE AGAINST SIN is serious business. It is, according to Zacharias Ursinus, a battle that requires us "to fight manfully against sin." Battling sin is not child's play; it is serious business where the stakes are eternal. If we do not put sin to death, it will rob us, loot us, maim us, and defeat us. "Sin," as an unnamed source said, "will take you farther than you want to go, keep you longer than you want to stay, and cost you more than you want to pay." In the end, if we don't put sin to death, it will decimate us. I have seen people over the years who are strong and invigorated be crippled and ultimately killed - all because of sin.

John Owen (1616-1683) writes, "Be killing sin or it will be killing you"[1] Owen continues, "The vigor, and power, and comfort of our spiritual life depends on the mortification of the deeds of the flesh."[2] J.I. Packer helps us understand the importance of a figure like John Owen and considers him "the greatest among Puritan theologians." Packer adds, "For solidity, profundity, massiveness and majesty in exhibiting from Scripture God's ways with sinful mankind there is no one to touch him."[3] We need towering figures like Owen; godly men who tell us the truth and lead us on a God-honoring and sin-destroying path.

Owen saw the problem of sin with fresh eyes that were attuned to Scripture. Packer sums up his view of sin:

> Sin within us, the anti-God drive in mankind's makeup that is our legacy from Adam, has noetic as well as behavioral consequences: it promises a universal unresponsiveness to spiritual truth and reality that the New Testament calls *hardness* and *blindness* of heart. Mere instruction thus proves ineffective; only the illumination of the Holy Spirit, opening our heart to God's word and God's word to our hearts, can bring understanding of, conviction about, and consent to, the things that God declares.[4]

When the apostle Paul penned his letter to the Christians in Colossae, he addressed a group, some of whom were straying from the gospel path. These people were duped into believing they could finish the Christian race and discover true spirituality through human philosophy (Col. 2:8), legalism (Col. 2:6-17), mystical experience (Col. 2:18), and asceticism (Col. 2:21-23). Some of the Colossian Christians had been side-tracked by sin.

Two thousand years later, Christians can identify with these people. It is so easy to get hoodwinked by the philosophy of the world, not to mention some of false ideas that have grown popular in the church like the "health and wealth gospel." Some Christians get side-tracked by legalism, believing with all their hearts that their efforts and obedience will win God's favor. Some get deceived by embracing a mystical approach to the Christian life, where the written revelation of God is ignored at best or discounted at worst. And some are paralyzed by the gnostic notion that suggests the body is evil and must therefore be neglected or punished in order to achieve true spirituality.

The apostle Paul cautions the Colossians and commends them to Christ who is supreme above all. In Colossians 3, his caution turns to counsel as he sets forth the training principles for dealing with sin.

As we get closer to the finish line, our goal in this chapter is to learn how to establish settled convictions in the Christian life. Establishing godly convictions, then, will set us on a trajectory for killing sin.

REAFFIRMING THE REALITY

In Colossians 3:1, Paul says, "If then you have been raised with Christ, seek the things that are above, where Christ is, seated at the right hand of God." Reaffirming the reality of our position in Christ is an essential ingredient in our battle against sin. Sinclair Ferguson comments:

> Failure to deal with the presence of sin can often be traced back to spiritual amnesia - forgetting our new, true, real identity. As a believer, I am someone who has been delivered from the dominion of sin and who therefore is free and motivated to fight against the remnants of sin in my heart. You must know, rest in, think through, and act upon your new identity - you are in Christ.[5]

Three principles help us reaffirm the reality of who we are in Christ. First, *we have been buried with Christ in baptism*. Scripture says, "We were buried therefore with him by baptism into death, in order that, just as Christ was raised from the dead by the glory of the Father, we too might walk in newness of life" (Rom. 6:4). We are no longer under the reign of sin. Sin, that diabolical monster no longer dominates our lives. Since we are no longer under the monstrous reign of sin, we live in an entirely new domain. We live under the domain of grace!

Second, *we have died with Christ*. Romans 6:6 says, "We know that our old self was crucified with him in order that the body of sin might be brought to nothing, so that we would no longer be enslaved to sin." Our old self was crucified with Christ. "Let us never again try to get rid of the old man," writes Lloyd-Jones. He continues, "This is something we are to believe, and to receive by faith. This is not something you experience, this is something you believe; and it is only as you believe it that your experience will be triumphant."[6]

Additionally, the Bible tells us that the body of sin is "brought to nothing." Lloyd Jones continues, "The old man has gone. I am no longer that man; I am a new man in Christ Jesus. That is what is true about me. But though that is the truth about me, it is not yet the truth about my body, my mortal body. Sin is still in my mortal body, in my members, working as 'a law in my members,' having its effect upon my 'instruments,' 'my members,' the parts of my body."[7] There is a distinction, then, between the old man and the body of sin. The old man has been crucified with Christ; the body of sin (or the flesh) may still be influenced by sin. "The body is not inherently sinful but sin does have the power over the body even in the man who is 'in Christ.' The man himself is delivered, but his body is not yet delivered, and that is why the Apostle says, 'We are waiting for adoption."[8]

Some people have wondered if the "body of sin" in verse 6 is literally *destroyed*. This is precisely how the King James Version translated the Greek verb, *katargeithei*. But this is a misunderstanding. This word is properly translated as "rendered idle, inactive, or deprived of force or power." Accordingly, the ESV translates this word, "brought to nothing." The CSB most accurately reflects the meaning of *katargeithei*:

> For we know that our old self was crucified with him so that the body ruled by sin might be rendered powerless (katargeithei*)* so that we may no longer be enslaved to sin. (Rom. 6:6, CSB)

In other words, believers are released from the controlling power of sin. We are no longer compelled to submit to the tyrannical demands of sin.

Third, *we have been raised with Christ*. Paul writes, "In him also you were circumcised with a circumcision made without hands, by putting off the body of the flesh, by the circumcision of Christ, having been buried with him in baptism, in which you were also raised with him through faith in the powerful working of God, who raised him from the dead" (Col. 2:11–12). The verb translated as *raised* means "to raise together; to raise up together from mortal death to a life that is dedicated in a fresh way to God."

> ... even when we were dead in our trespasses, made us alive together with Christ—by grace you have been saved— and raised us up with him and seated us with him in the heavenly places in Christ Jesus. (Eph. 2:5–6)
>
> For if we have been united with him in a death like his, we shall certainly be united with him in a resurrection like his. (Rom.6:5)

The same power that the Father used to gloriously raise the Son from the dead is operating in us! "What is true of His death is true of us, what is true of His burial is true of us, and what is true of His resurrection is true of us."[9]

The implications of these great gospel realities are nothing short of breathtaking. First, *when you are tempted to sin, remember - you have the power to say NO!* Lloyd-Jones is quick to remind us, "I died with him, I was buried with him, I rose with him; I am in the new realm. It is a new life altogether. As he has finished with the rule and reign and the realm of sin completely and absolutely, so have we also."[10]

Second, *we have been raised from death to life*. "True religion," writes Jonathan Edwards, "in great part, consists in holy affec tions."[11] Our desires have changed. Our delights have changed. What once brought pleasure, now seems putrid. What once seemed rewarding is now rancid. Since we have been raised with Christ, our inclinations have been utterly transformed. Our affections have been renewed, renovated, and reformed! While we are free from the penalty of sin and the power of sin, the battle will not end until we are glorified. But until that great day, we must reaffirm the reality of who we are in Christ.

THE RESPONSE

The response, of course, must be biblical in scope. Paul writes, "If then you have been raised with Christ, seek the things that are above, where Christ is, seated at the right hand of God" (Col. 3:1).

We must seek things that are above

To *seek* (zeitéō) means "to seek by thinking, meditating, reasoning; to crave or demand something or someone." Seeking involves diligently striving after and pursuing God. A.W. Tozer reminds us that a failure to pursue God leads to disastrous results:

> The stiff and wooden quality about our religious lives is a result of a lack of our holy desire. Complacency is a deadly foe of all spiritual growth. Acute desire must be present or there will be

> no manifestation of Christ to His people ... The shallowness of our inner experience, the hollowness of our worship, and that servile imitation of the world which marks our promotional methods all testify that we, in this day, know God only imperfectly, and the peace of God scarcely at all.[12]

David models what this longing for God looks like: "One thing have I asked of the LORD, that I will seek after: that I may dwell in the house of the LORD all the days of my life, to gaze upon the beauty of the LORD and to inquire in his temple" (Ps. 27:4).

Seeking things above is a command. Seeking things above must be persistent. And seeking things above involves cultivating an eternal perspective where the City of God supplants the City of Man; where God's values replace values established by the world; where God's Word replaces the musings of man. The sphere of our seeking is above, where Christ is, seated at the right hand of the Father.

Several examples of what it means to seek may be found in the New Testament. Jesus calls the people of God to seek first his kingdom and righteousness (Matt. 6:33). In the parable of the lost coin, we find a woman who diligently seeks (Luke 15:8). And Zacchaeus seeks Jesus (Luke 19:3).

We must set our minds on things above

Paul writes, "Set your minds on things that are above, not on things that are on earth" (Col. 3:2). *Phronéō*, the Greek term, which is translated set means "to have understanding; to be wise; to direct one's mind to a thing; to seek or strive after." Setting our minds on things above involves concentration and deep thinking. Setting our minds on things above is a command. Setting our minds on things above must be persistent. And setting our minds on things above involves cultivating an eternal perspective. "A prime mark of the Christian mind is that it cultivates the eternal perspective," writes Harry Blamires.[13] Jonathan Edwards prayed, "Stamp eternity on my eyeballs."

Setting our minds on things above means that our minds must be occupied with things that glorify God:

> Finally, brothers, whatever is true, whatever is honorable, whatever is just, whatever is pure, whatever is lovely, whatever is commendable, if there is any excellence, if there is anything worthy of praise, think about these things. (Phil. 4:8)

Setting our minds on things above involves longing for the coming of Christ. "... So Christ, having been offered once to bear the sins of many, will appear a second time, not to deal with sin but to save those who are eagerly waiting for him" (Heb. 9:28).

Preoccupation with the world (or earthly things) prevents us from obeying these imperatives in Colossians 3:1-2. Beware of investing large amounts of time in the little things and a little amount of time in the big things. The psalmist adds, "So teach us to number our days that we may get a heart of wisdom" (Ps. 90:12). We have a divine perspective on life. We have a divine perspective on Providence. We understand the big picture and see that God and his kingdom purposes are being carried out according to his all-wise decree.

So, we establish settled convictions concerning eternity by reaffirming the reality, by responding biblically, and by recognizing the rationale behind counsel.

THE RATIONALE

"For you have died, and your life is hidden with Christ in God. When Christ who is your life appears, then you also will appear with him in glory" (Col. 3:3–4). We are in vital union with Christ (Gal. 2:20). We are secure in our relationship with him. Nothing can separate us from the love of Christ (Rom. 8:38-39). And we will appear with Christ in glory. The world does not understand or recognize our union with Christ. Our life is hidden with Christ. At his second coming, everything will become clear. We will appear with him in glory!

Have you established settled convictions? Are you reaffirming the reality that you have been raised with Christ? Are you responding biblically by seeking the things that are above and setting your mind on things above? And have you recognized the rationale that you are in vital union with Christ, that your relationship is eternally secure and one day, you will appear with him in glory?

Oh, reader, may God grant you the ability, by his Spirit to develop settled convictions concerning eternal things so that you will be in a position to win the race. May you lay aside every weight, and the sin which clings so closely, and run the race that is set before you, looking to Jesus, the founder and perfecter of your faith (Heb. 12:1-2). And with settled convictions, may you be killing sin.

---

1. John Owen, Temptation and Sin (Edinburgh: Banner of Truth, 1950-1953), 6:9.
2. Ibid.
3. J.I. Packer, The Quest for Godliness (Wheaton: Crossway Books, 1990), 81.
4. Ibid., 83.
5. Sinclair Ferguson, In Christ Alone (Orlando: Reformation Trust Publishing, 2007), 219.

6. Martyn Lloyd-Jones, Romans 6: The New Man (Edinburgh: Banner of Truth, 1972), 65.
7. Ibid., 65.
8. Ibid., 75.
9. Ibid., 52.
10. Ibid.
11. The Works of Jonathan Edwards, Religious Affections, ed. John E. Smith (New Haven: Yale University Press, 1959), 2:95.
12. A.W. Tozer, The Pursuit of God (Camp Hill: Christian Publications, Inc. 1982), 17-18.
13. Harry Blamires, The Christian Mind: How Should a Christian Think? (Ann Arbor: Servant Publications, 1963), 67.

14

Be Killing Sin

There is more power in the death of Christ to conquer sin and Satan than in all the intelligence and self-denial of man.

JOEL BEEKE

We are engaged in an epic battle that doesn't end until death. Therefore, we must engage in holy warfare. Sun Tzu acknowledged the importance of warfare and the careful deliberations that lead to a successful outcome: "Now the general who wins the battle makes many calculations in his temple ere the battle is fought. The general who loses a battle makes but few calculations beforehand. Thus do many calculations lead to victory, and a few calculations to defeat: how much more no calculation at all! It is by attention to this point that I can foresee who is likely to win or lose."[1] This battle is spiritual in nature and is unrelenting. Much is at stake as we wage war with sin. In his letter to the church at Rome, Paul the apostle addresses the matter of indwelling sin:

> Now if I do what I do not want, it is no longer I who do it, but sin that dwells within me. So I find it to be a law that when I want to do right, evil lies close at hand. For I delight in the law of God, in

> my inner being, but I see in my members another law waging war against the law of my mind and making me captive to the law of sin that dwells in my members. Wretched man that I am! Who will deliver me from this body of death? Thanks be to God through Jesus Christ our Lord! So then, I myself serve the law of God with my mind, but with my flesh I serve the law of sin. (Rom. 7:20–25)

Where does sin indwell? It dwells inside each of us. Paul calls it a law. Kris Lundgaard writes:

> In what sense has Christ defeated sin in the believer? The answer is that he has overthrown its rule, weakened its power, and even killed its root so that it cannot bear the fruit of eternal death in the believer. Sin is sin; its nature and purpose remain unchanged; its force and success still grab us by the throat.[2]

The force of indwelling sin is both vicious and relentless. Indeed, it is like a perpetual battering ram that hammers away with brute force. John Owen describes the battle that each Christian faces: "Any thing, state, way, or condition, that upon any account whatsoever, has a force or efficacy to seduce, to draw the mind and heart of a man from its obedience, which God requires of him, into any sin, in any degree of it whatsoever."[3]

What kinds of things in this world seduce us or draw our minds and hearts from obeying God and treasuring his promises? Owen continues to probe:

> In particular, that is a temptation to any man which causes or occasions him to sin, or in anything to go off from his duty, either by bringing evil into his heart, or drawing out that evil that is in his heart, or any other way diverting him from communion with God and that constant, equal, universal obedience (emphasis mine) in matter and manner, that is required of him.[4]

Universal obedience. These words should jump off the page and capture our attention. For when we consider sin and temptation, we need to understand what God is after. He is after our hearts. He is looking for obedient men and women.

> For the eyes of the LORD run to and fro throughout the whole earth, to give strong support to those whose heart is blameless toward him. You have done foolishly in this, for from now on you will have wars. (2 Chron. 16:9)

> And Samuel said, 'Has the LORD as great delight in burnt offerings and sacrifices, as in obeying the voice of the LORD? Behold, to obey is better than sacrifice, and to listen than the fat of rams. For rebellion is as the sin of divination, and presumption is as iniquity and idolatry. Because you have rejected the word of the LORD, he has also rejected you from being king.' (1 Sam. 15:22–23)

Do you desire to obey God? Do you delight in obeying him? Wrestling with your deepest motivations are paramount at this point. What is your heart's desire and why? What are some of the deepest longings in your life? These are the kinds of questions we must wrestle with as we engage in holy warfare.

Several years ago, I sat at a coffee shop with a man who was raised in a background that was prone to legalism. He proudly rolled up his sleeve to showcase a tattoo he received to remind him of those days, which were characterized by a lopsided view of law and grace, at least from his vantage point. His experience led him to a conclusion which is fundamentally flawed. He stated his position with a grin on his face: "There are no imperatives in the New Testament," he said.

To be fair, my friend was earnestly trying to guard against earning salvation via law-keeping. His inner inclination was to react strongly to the legalism of his younger days. And he was fearful of neglecting the gospel and placing an unhealthy emphasis on the law.

The chief problem with my friend's conclusion is this: He was dead wrong. He not only failed to distinguish between law and gospel; he forgot that the New Testament is packed with imperatives. Kevin DeYoung comments, "There is nothing sub-Christian in talking about obedience to God's commands. There is nothing inherently anti-gospel in being exhorted to keep the imperatives of Scripture. There is nothing ungracious about divine demands. Just the opposite, in fact - there is grace in getting law."[5] My friend fell prey to the lie that the law has no purpose, whatsoever!

The reality is this: the Bible contains indicatives (what God has done) and imperatives (what God commands us to do or not do). "Both the indicatives of Scripture and the imperatives are from God, for our good, and given in grace."[6] Here is the chief lesson: indicatives fuel imperatives. John MacArthur adds, "All biblical exhortations to believers are based on the blessings and promises they already have from the Lord. Without the provisions we have from Him, we would be unable to fulfill the commands we receive from him."[7] In other words, indicatives fuel imperatives.

If you are a Christian, pray a prayer like this: "God would you please bring to mind the sins in my life that need to be extinguished." Perhaps you battle with sins of the mind. Or maybe you struggle with sins of the heart. Perhaps you wrestle with sins of the flesh. Whatever the case may be, John Owen's warning is appropriate: "Every unclean thought or glance would be adultery if it could; every covetous desire would be oppression, every thought of unbelief would be atheism ..."[8] What are the sins that prevent you from moving forward in the Christian life? What kinds of things in this world seduce you or draw your mind and heart away from obeying God? Again, much is at stake! John Owen reminds us, "The contest is for our lives and souls."[9]

God is looking for obedient people (2 Chron. 16:9). God is calling his people to live distinctly. One of the best ways of living distinctly is by dealing with sin directly. Romans 8:12-13 arms us to do this very thing:

> So then, brothers, we are debtors, not to the flesh, to live according to the flesh. For if you live according to the flesh you will die, but if by the Spirit you put to death the deeds of the body, you will live.

The importance of this passage cannot be overstated. John Owen adds, "The choicest believers, who are assuredly freed from the condemning power of sin, ought yet to make it their business all their days to mortify the indwelling power of sin."[10] Or more simply, *Christians are commanded to put sin to death.*

Romans 8:12 tells us that "we are debtors, not to the flesh, to living according to the flesh." A debtor is "a person who is under moral obligation to do something." We are no longer obligated to the tyranny of sin. Sin is not what defines us. We have no obligations to the flesh.

In verse 13, Paul leads us onto the "firing range." Notice three bullet points (pun intended); each of which will be stated in the form of a question that will enable us to put sin to death:

For if you live according to the flesh you will die, but if by the Spirit you put to death the deeds of the body, you will live. (Rom. 8:13)

WHY DO WE NEED TO PUT SIN TO DEATH?

First, *sin leads to judgment*. I want to draw your attention to a particular word in Romans 8:13. It is the word will (*méllete*). Here is a word that means *certainty*. In other words, there is no ambiguity here. You have no doubt heard it said, "The only thing certain in life is death and taxes." You can add *spiritual death* to that list. Scripture is emphatic on this point:

> Behold, all souls are mine; the soul of the father as well as the soul of the son is mine: the soul who sins shall die. (Ezek.18:4)
>
> For to set the mind on the flesh is death, but to set the mind on the Spirit is life and peace. (Rom. 8:6)
>
> Put to death therefore what is earthly in you: sexual immorality, impurity, passion, evil desire, and covetousness, which is idolatry. On account of these the wrath of God is coming. (Col. 3:5–6)
>
> For the wages of sin is death, but the free gift of God is eternal life in Christ Jesus our Lord. (Rom. 6:23)

Second, *apart from mortification, we drift into a state of sloth.* Donald Whitney writes:

> The flesh, our natural inclination toward sin, does not contribute to our spiritual growth. Unless 'by the Spirit' we *labor* to 'put to death the deeds of the body' (Romans 8:13), our progress in godliness will be very slow. Unless we find *practical* ways to fight against our congenital tendency toward spiritual sloth, and pray for the Holy Spirit's power upon those practical ways, we will not build ourselves up in the faith (see Jude 20); we will drift toward spiritual entropy instead.[11]

This spiritual sloth will continue to spiral in a downward state unless we choose to consciously kill sin by the power of the Spirit.

Third, *sin no longer dominates our lives or dictates how we live.* Again, the Scriptures clearly articulate this point:

> In these you too once walked, when you were living in them. But now you must put them all away: anger, wrath, malice, slander, and obscene talk from your mouth. (Col. 3:7–8)

> We were buried therefore with him by baptism into death, in order that, just as Christ was raised from the dead by the glory of the Father, we too might walk in newness of life. (Rom. 6:4)

> We know that our old self was crucified with him in order that the body of sin might be brought to nothing, so that we would no longer be enslaved to sin. For one who has died has been set free from sin. (Rom. 6:6–7)

We put sin to death because sin leads to judgment. And since we are followers of Christ, sin no longer dominates our lives or dictates how we live. Pay close attention to several practical steps we must take in order to remind ourselves of the importance of putting sin to death.

APPLICATION

1. **We live with holy fear**

We live with the full understanding that the end result of sin is death. "For if you live according to the flesh you will die" (Rom. 8:13a). Two Puritan pastors speak candidly about this important matter:

> Love will be apt to grow wanton if it is not poised by with holy fear. No better curb or antidote against sin than fear. If we could see hell fire in every sin, it would make us fear to commit it.[12]
>
> Mark it, the face of the Lord. What is God's face? It is the manifestation of Himself and His glorious attributes. The face of the Lord is against them that do evil. Oh, that you would consider this, you who do evil, whose conscience cannot but tell you that you do evil. Know that the face of God is against you, and is this nothing to have the face of God against you? The face of God is terrible in the world when He meets with a sinner. One sight of the face of God against a soul cannot but overwhelm the soul and sink it down to the bottomless gulf of despair, if God does not hold him by His mighty hand. There is much terror in it.[13]

2. **We live with holy obligation**

Why did God choose a people for his own possession? Why did God elect a people in eternity past?

> even as he chose us in him before the foundation of the world, that we should be holy and blameless before him ... (Eph. 1:4)
>
> By this my Father is glorified, that you bear much fruit and so prove to be my disciples. (John 15:8)
>
> These things I have spoken to you, that my joy may be in you, and that your joy may be full. (John 15:11)
>
> You did not choose me, but I chose you and appointed you that you should go and bear fruit and that your fruit should abide, so that whatever you ask the Father in my name, he may give it to you. (John 15:16)
>
> For God has not called us for impurity, but in holiness. (1 Thess. 4:7)

And so, we are not obligated to the flesh; we are obligated to operate in a new realm. We are called to live according to the Spirit (Gal. 5:16). We are obligated to the Spirit. As God's chosen people, we are obligated to live godly lives!

3. **We live with holy power**

In Romans 8:1-11, the apostle Paul describes how the Holy Spirit enables us to live in victory over sin. The Spirit of God dwells in us (Rom. 8:9-11). That is, we have divine resources to live the Christian life; resources that did not exist before our conversion.

4. **We live with holy motivation**

"If you live according to the flesh you will die" (Rom. 8:13). This is a principle that should be well-ingrained in our hearts and minds by this point. For Adam was warned that if he transgressed the law of God, he would die (Gen. 2:17). Therefore, we live with holy motivation. We strive to please our Commanding Officer. We strive to glorify the Lord Jesus Christ in everything we say and do.

WHAT KIND OF SIN DO WE KILL?

What kind of sin do we kill as followers of Jesus Christ? Of course, the obvious answer is all sin - in every size, shape, and color. But Paul gets specific in two important passages. In Romans 8:13, he instructs us to "put to death the deeds of the body." *Deeds* (*praăxis*) is "any specific behavior or purposeful activity."

In Colossians 3:5-6 Paul instructs us to "put to death therefore what is earthly in you: sexual immorality, impurity, passion, evil desire, and covetousness, which is idolatry. On account of these the wrath of God is coming."

Sexual immorality (*porneia*) - "sexual acts that are morally objectionable."

> For out of the heart come evil thoughts, murder, adultery, sexual immorality, theft, false witness, slander. (Matt. 15:19)

> Flee from sexual immorality. Every other sin a person commits is outside the body, but the sexually immoral person sins against his own body. (1 Cor. 6:18)

> Now the works of the flesh are evident: sexual immorality, impurity, sensuality, idolatry, sor-

cery, enmity, strife, jealousy, fits of anger, rivalries, dissensions, divisions. (Gal. 5:19–20)

But sexual immorality and all impurity or covetousness must not even be named among you, as is proper among saints. (Eph. 5:3)

For this is the will of God, your sanctification: that you abstain from sexual immorality; that each one of you know how to control his own body in holiness and honor ... (1 Thess. 4:3–4)

Impurity (*àkatharsia*) - "Immorality; filth."

Therefore God gave them up in the lusts of their hearts to *impurity*, to the dishonoring of their bodies among themselves. (Rom. 1:24)

Now the works of the flesh are evident: sexual immorality, impurity, sensuality, idolatry, sorcery, enmity, strife, jealousy, fits of anger, rivalries, dissensions, divisions. (Gal. 5:19–20)

They have become callous and have given themselves up to sensuality, greedy to practice every kind of *impurity*. (Eph. 4:19)

For God has not called us for *impurity*, but in holiness. (1 Thess. 4:7)

Passion (*páthos*) - "Strong feeling or emotion; lustful passion."

> For this reason God gave them up to dishonorable passions. For their women exchanged natural relations for those that are contrary to nature ... (Rom. 1:26)

> For this is the will of God, your sanctification: that you abstain from sexual immorality; that each one of you know how to control his own body in holiness and honor, not in the passion of lust like the Gentiles who do not know God ... (1 Thess. 4:3-5)

Evil desire (*kakós épithumía*) - "Evil craving; a self-indulgence that dethrones God."

> But put on the Lord Jesus Christ, and make no provision for the flesh, to gratify its desires. (Rom. 13:14)

> But I say, walk by the Spirit, and you will not gratify the desires of the flesh. (Gal. 5:16)

> And those who belong to Christ Jesus have crucified the flesh with its passions and desires. (Gal. 5:24)

> ... to put off your old self, which belongs to your former manner of life and is corrupt through deceitful desires ... (Eph. 4:22)

Covetousness (*pleonexía*) - "Greediness; the compulsive desire to attain my worldly pleasures."

Idolatry (*eidōlolatría*) - "The worship of a material representation of deity."

Calvin gets to the heart of the matter when he refers to man's nature as "a perpetual factory of idols."[14] Remember, we are no longer obligated to the tyranny of sin. Sin is not what defines us as regenerate people who have been cleansed by the blood of Christ. We have no obligations to the flesh. Yet, we continue to battle sin. Our holy warfare with sin does not end until we breath our last.

I recently heard a story about a man who walked out to his backyard to stretch his tired muscles after a strenuous workout. A raven was sitting on his fence making a horrible, screeching sound. He noticed the bird would look up at him, then look down. As he walked closer to the screeching raven, he noticed a rattlesnake moving under the fence. After "taking care" of the snake, the man proceeded to describe how fascinated he was with that crazy bird. He said, "I really think the raven was warning me. Maybe God put that instinct in the bird. Perhaps God used that part of his creation to once again prove his love for me." But then the man had a second thought. "The next time your pastor is preaching about a particular sin and all you hear is him screeching, maybe you should pay attention. Maybe your pastor sees the deadly snake in the grass."

We have identified several snakes in the grass in this book. My hope is that you have heard the raven crowing - loudly. My prayer is that you will take appropriate action by putting sin to death!

HOW DO WE PUT SIN TO DEATH?

Finally, we come to the critical question that focuses on the responsibility for killing sin. How do we put sin to death? Or better yet, exactly who is responsible for mortifying sin? Does the Holy Spirit mortify sin or do Christians bear this weighty responsibility? The answer is, "Yes!" Notice four principles that will set us on a path of victory:

1. **Killing sin requires a decisive resolution**

Scripture says:

> Put to death therefore what is earthly in you: sexual immorality, impurity, passion, evil desire, and covetousness, which is idolatry. On account of these the wrath of God is coming. (Col. 3:5–6)
>
> For if you live according to the flesh you will die, but if by the Spirit you put to death the deeds of the body, you will live. (Rom. 8:13)

Put to death (*nekros*) means "to stop a state or activity with lethal determination; to put something to death" - in this case, sin. *Put to death* is the key; and it deserves our special attention. The phrase *put to death* is an aorist tense verb, which indicates point in time action. It is a command that we are obligated to obey. John MacArthur adds, "Believers are to make a decisive resolution to put sin to death, bring the flesh under subjection to the Spirit-filled disposition."[15] Now is the time to get serious about sin. The stakes couldn't be any higher. Now is the time to make a decisive resolution.

2. **Killing sin requires an obedient constitution**

Obedient followers of Christ keep in step with the Spirit. Paul writes, "But I say, walk by the Spirit, and you will not gratify the desires of the flesh" (Gal. 5:16). So we walk in humble dependence upon the Spirit and his leading. We walk properly and put on the Lord Jesus Christ. "Let us walk properly as in the daytime, not in orgies and drunkenness, not in sexual immorality and sensuality, not in quarreling and jealousy. But put on the Lord Jesus Christ, and make no provision for the flesh, to gratify its desires" (Rom. 13:13-14). John Owen adds, "Holiness is nothing but the implanting, writing and relishing of the gospel in our souls."[16] Our passion as followers of Christ is to remain steadfast and true. Killing sin, then, requires an obedient constitution.

3. **Killing sin requires daily participation**

Paul is emphatic on this point: " ... But if by the Spirit you put to death the deeds of the body, you will live" (Rom. 8:13). *Thanatòō* is the Greek verb translated as "put to death." This is a present imperative verb, which suggests ongoing activity. In other words, putting sin to death is a daily responsibility for every Christ-follower.

What steps can you take this week to "put to death the deeds of the body?" What habits need to be eliminated? What habits need fine tuning? And positively, what habits need to begin? Which of the habits below need to be included in your regular routine?

- Reading Scripture (Ps. 1:1-6)
- Meditating on Scripture (Ps. 119:15)
- Memorizing Scripture (Ps. 119:11)
- Focused prayer (1 Thess. 5:17)
- Accountable relationships (Prov. 27:17)

Who can stand with you and encourage you as you commit to putting sin to death on a daily basis? As important as accountable relationships are, your most important ally in your fight against sin is the Lord Jesus Christ. Isaac Ambrose writes,

> Nothing will purify the heart, and mortify sin, like looking unto Jesus, in his love, agonies, and death. If God mercifully delivers you from the power of your inbred corruptions, and the snares

> of the devil, and blesses you with a pure heart, and a quiet mind, spend the remainder of your days on earth in gratitude to God for such peculiar favors.[17]

Constantly turn your attention to the Son of God and his cross. Thomas Watson adds, "So take these three darts - the Word of God, prayer, and mortification - and strike through the heart of your lusts so that they die."[18] But killing sin is not an activity that we engage in alone. We need divine help. We need the Holy Spirit.

4. **Killing sin requires consistent trust in the Holy Spirit**

John Owen writes, "The vigor, and power, and comfort of our spiritual life depends on the mortification of the deeds of the flesh."[19] Paul's final point in verse 13 requires an ever-deepening faith. He writes, " ... *but if by the Spirit* you put to death the deeds of the body, you will live." The only way we will kill sin is to trust in the power of the Holy Spirit. The fight against sin, therefore, is a fight to trust God. The fight against sin is a fight to trust the promises of God. Indeed, the fight against sin requires that we bank everything on the mighty reality of the gospel!

Mortification is not a method; it is a mindset. In his treatment of the mortification of sin, Ray Ortlund Jr. adds, "It is faith at work. It is a determination to stop dying and start living in the fulness of the Spirit. It is a hungering and thirsting for righteousness so much that we act boldly and lay hold of it, looking to the Lord moment by moment for his strength."[20] This is one of the many reasons why legalism simply will not work. Legalism will never sanctify us. Legalism will never assist us in the Christian life. Legalism will never help mortify our sin. God prescribes one way of dealing with sin; it must be decisively killed by the power of the Holy Spirit. And when you submit to Scripture by putting to death the deeds of the body, the result, according to Romans 8:13 is life. In other words, obedience in this area leads to a supernatural life!

The Heidelberg Catechism asks:

> Question: *How many things are necessary for you to know, that you in this comfort may live and die happily?*
>
> Answer: Three things. First the greatness of my sin and misery. Second, how I am redeemed from all my sins and miseries. Third, how I am to be thankful to God for such redemption.[21]

For the Skeptical or Unbelieving

If you have not yet received God's free gift of salvation by grace alone through faith alone in Jesus Christ, the question before you is very grave. If you are not yet a Christian, you must ask:

> "What sins have I committed against a holy God?"
>
> "On what basis will my sins be forgiven?"

You must come to grips with the most important reality in the universe: Your only hope is the gospel of the Lord Jesus Christ. The gospel is summarized in Paul's letter to the church in Corinth:

> Now I would remind you, brothers, of the gospel I preached to you, which you received, in which

> you stand, and by which you are being saved, if you hold fast to the word I preached to you—unless you believed in vain. For I delivered to you as of first importance what I also received: that Christ died for our sins in accordance with the Scriptures, that he was buried, that he was raised on the third day in accordance with the Scriptures, and that he appeared to Cephas, then to the twelve. (1 Cor. 15:1–5)

The Lord Jesus Christ lived the life that you could never live. He was tempted in every way, but he never sinned. He died a horrifying death on a cross that you deserve to die. The Bible says that your sins have created a massive chasm between you and a holy God: "It's your sins that have cut you off from God. Because of your sins, he has turned away and will not listen anymore" (Isa. 59:2, NLT). Romans 6:23 says, "For the wages of sin is death, but the free gift of God is eternal life in Christ Jesus our Lord."

The good news is that Jesus came to redeem sinners (Titus 2:14). He came to destroy the works of the devil (1 John 3:8). He came to reconcile sinners to a holy God (Rom. 5:10). Jesus came to bring us into his kingdom by dying for the sins of everyone who would ever believe. He took our punishment; he stood in our place; he bore the wrath of God for every person who would ever believe:

> For our sake he made him to be sin who knew no sin, so that in him we might become the righteousness of God. (2 Cor. 5:21)

Because of his death on the cross, and his resurrection three days later, the Bible can say:

> He has delivered us from the domain of darkness and transferred us to the kingdom of his beloved Son, in whom we have redemption, the forgiveness of sins. (Col. 1:13–14)

One day, the Lord Jesus Christ will return gloriously and usher in a kingdom where every wrong will be overturned. Our Savior will make all things new!

And so, Jesus Christ is your only hope. Jesus is the only one qualified to extinguish your sins. Jesus Christ is the only one qualified to forgive your sins - past, present, and future:

> And there is salvation in no one else, for there is no other name under heaven given among men by which we must be saved. (Acts 4:12)

As we draw to a close, you are faced with the most important decision you'll ever make. You must consider your standing before a holy God, for you will stand before him on judgment day. You must turn from your sin and turn to the Lord Jesus Christ in order to receive forgiveness and eternal life.

Acts 16:31 says, "Believe in the Lord Jesus, and you will be saved ..." At first glance, this appears to be an important invitation. Indeed, this is the most important invitation that you will ever receive. This is an invitation to bow before the Lord of the universe. It is an invitation to submit to his authority. This is an invitation to trust in his kingly reign and walk with him in obedience.

But Acts 16:31 is more than a mere invitation. This is a divine command! And this command is binding upon every person.

The apostle Paul proclaimed the gospel to the philosophers in Acts 17. Listen to the divine summons:

> ... This I proclaim to you. The God who made the world and everything in it, being Lord of heaven and earth, does not live in temples made by man, nor is he served by human hands, as though he needed anything, since he himself gives to all mankind life and breath and everything. (Acts 17:23–25)

The times of ignorance God overlooked, *but now he commands all people everywhere to repent*, because he has fixed a day on which he will judge the world in righteousness by a man whom he has appointed; and of this he has given assurance to all by raising him from the dead. (Acts 17:30–31)

Once again, you must ask:

> "What sins have I committed against a holy God?"
>
> "On what basis will my sins be forgiven?"

Jesus Christ is the only one qualified to forgive you and usher you into the presence of God. Will you turn from your sin and trust the Lord Jesus Christ today?

---

1. Sun Tzu, The Art of War, 9.
2. Kris Lundgaard, The Enemy Within (Phillipsburg: P&R, 1998), 24.

3. John Owen, Cited in Kelly M. Kapic and Justin Taylor, Overcoming Sin and Temptation (Wheaton: Crossway Books, 2006), 156.
4. Ibid., 156.
5. Kevin DeYoung, The Hole in Our Holiness (Wheaton: Crossway Books, 2012), 52.
6. Ibid., 55.
7. John MacArthur, The MacArthur New Testament Commentary - Romans 1-8 (Chicago: Moody Press, 1991), 421.
8. John Owen, Mortification of Sin in Believers, 12.
9. Ibid., 13.
10. John Owen, Of the Mortification of Sin in Believers, Temptation and Sin (Edinburgh: Banner of Truth, reprint 1850), 6:7.
11. Donald S. Whitney, Spiritual Disciplines for the Christian Life (Colorado Springs: NavPress, 1991, 2014), 264-265.
12. Watson, The Mischief of Sin, 41.
13. Jeremiah Burroughs, The Evil of Evils (Grand Rapids: Soli Deo Publications, reprint 1654), 147.
14. John Calvin, Institutes of the Christian Religion (Philadelphia: Westminster Press, reprint 1536), 108.
15. John MacArthur, The MacArthur New Testament Commentary - Colossians & Philemon (Chicago: Moody Press, 1992), 136.
16. John Owen, Cited in J.I. Packer, A Quest for Godliness: The Puritan Vision of the Christian Life (Wheaton: Crossway Books, 1990), 200.
17. Isaac Ambrose, The Christian Warrior: Wrestling with Sin, Satan, the World and the Flesh (Digital Puritan Press, 2012), Loc. 1453.
18. Watson, The Mischief of Sin, 51.
19. John Owen, Of the Mortification of Sin in Believers (Edinburgh: Banner of Truth, reprint 1967), 7.

20. Ray Ortlund Jr., Supernatural Living for Natural People: The Life-Giving Message of Romans 8 (Genies House: Christian Focus, 2001), 63.
21. The Heidelberg Catechism (Edinburgh: Banner of Truth, 2013), 10.

Conclusion

If you are a Christian, Paul makes it plain that we are no longer debtors to the flesh (Rom. 8:12). But we do have a new set of obligations, as we have seen. Christians are commanded to put sin to death by the power of the Spirit. John Calvin speaks about the mindset of a godly person and unlocks what proves to be an important key that we need to turn in our battle against sin:

> This mind restrains itself from sinning, not out of dread of punishment alone; but, because it loves and reveres God as Father, it worships and adores him as Lord. Even if there were no hell, it would still shudder at offending him alone.[1]

Sin should horrify every follower of Jesus Christ. Sin should repulse us. The object of our affection is the Lord Jesus Christ. The deepest desire of our hearts is to please and glorify him. This is why spiritual pacifism never works for Christians. Spiritual pacifism is never an option for a follower of Jesus Christ. In fact, spiritual pacifism is blatant idolatry and disobedience to Christ and his commands. We must, therefore, proactively and aggressively put sin to death, by the power of the Spirit.

Think about your life and the various sins you struggle with. Brothers and sisters, now is the time to fight! Calvin continues,

"The way forward for you and me - 'putting to death the deeds of the body' - is a rugged, take-no prisoners determination to stop pandering to the flesh and start afresh, no matter what the personal cost."[2] Joel Beeke and Gary Smalley write, "The Christian approach to sin is a combination of contrition and combat."[3] "We are not fighting to become free from the tyranny of sin but fighting because we are free."[4] So we humbly enter the battlefield, outfitted with spiritual armor, filled with God-centered resolve and fueled with biblical faith. We stand ready to fight.

What does this fight look like for you? How will you wage holy war against sin this week? This year? How will you wage war against sin for the rest of your days? Remember - the command to mortify sin is not a method - it is a mindset.

> For if you live according to the flesh you will die, but if by the Spirit you put to death the deeds of the body, you will live. (Rom. 8:13)

So, press on my dear brothers and sisters. Be killing sin! We have been granted supernatural resources to live the Christian life. We have received the indwelling Holy Spirit to strengthen our hands, mobilize our feet, embolden our lips, and sanctify our affections. And we have the Word of God, the sword of the Spirit as a powerful offensive weapon that we will wield in our battle against sin. Take heart. Be of good courage. The penalty of sin has been defeated. The power of sin has been vanquished. And the presence of sin will soon be a distant memory.

Soli Deo gloria!

---

1. Calvin, Institutes of the Christian Religion, 43.
2. Ibid.

3. Joel Beeke and Gary Smalley, Reformed Systematic Theology - Volume 2: Man and Christ (Wheaton: Crossway Books, 2020), 406.
4. Joel Beeke and Gary Smalley, Reformed Systematic Theology - Volume 3: Spirit and Salvation (Wheaton: Crossway Books, 2021), 678.

Acknowledgments

This book would never have been written were it not for some key people who have taught me the importance of killing sin and encouraged my Christian growth along the way.

My parents, Dr. David and Valaura Steele have always upheld the Word of God and urged me to walk in a way that pleases the Lord. They have also encouraged me to continue writing. Their constant affirmation keeps this author motivated.

My uncle, Paul Steele was my pastor as a child and Dr. Dwight Steele was my pastor in college. Their godly examples and constant pleas to walk in the Spirit were clearly heard and I trust have been heeded.

Pastor Wayne Pickens helped me fight the fight of faith for over eleven years as we served on staff at First Baptist Church in La Grande, Oregon. Wayne helped me stand strong, even in the darkest days. I'll always cherish our friendship and look back on our ministry years together with God-centered nostalgia.

Dr. David Craig stood in the trenches with me during college and even though we live in different states, he continues to be a faithful fellow foot- soldier, praying, admonishing, and encouraging - all the way to the Celestial City.

Dr. Jon Volz has been a constant source of encouragement for over forty years. He has walked with me and wrestled with deep theological issues, sharpening my mind and shaping my heart.

Ron Coia is never afraid to ask honest questions, make bold suggestions, and constantly holds my feet to the fire.

My wife Gerrene is constantly at my side encouraging me to write and shepherd the flock. I love her more than anything in this world!

Tim Spencer, Daryl Groves, and Pastor Bruce Parker labored over the manuscript and offered several helpful suggestions. Their sharp editorial eyes and keen theological minds were greatly appreciated.

About Author

DR. DAVID S. STEELE has been in pastoral ministry since 1991. He holds BS and MA degrees from Multnomah University and Multnomah Biblical Seminary and a D. Min from Bakke Graduate University. Following graduation from Multnomah University, he served eight years as Pastor to Students at Lacey Chapel. In 2000, he became the Pastor of Theology at First Baptist Church in La Grande, Oregon where he served for over eleven years. In 2012, he became the Senior Pastor at Christ Fellowship in Everson, Washington.

At Christ Fellowship he leads the staff, serves as the Pastor for preaching and vision casting, and oversees *Veritas* (Adult Theological Education) and *Iron Men* (Men's Leadership Development).

His personal mission is to positively influence people, impact the world one person at a time and to glorify God by enjoying him forever. His passion in ministry is preaching, teaching, writing, and leadership development. Specifically, his aim is to educate the mind, engage the affections, equip the whole person, and encourage God-centered living that treasures Christ above all things.

He and his wife, Gerrene were married in 1991 and they have two children.

Made in the USA
Middletown, DE
14 March 2024

50834468R00126